The Fabian Society

The Fabian Society is Britain's leading left of centre think tank and political society, committed to creating the political ideas and policy debates which can shape the future of progressive politics.

With over 300 Fabian MPs, MEPs, Peers, MSPs and AMs, the Society plays an unparalleled role in linking the ability to influence policy debates at the highest level with vigorous grassroots debate among our growing membership of over 7000 people, 70 local branches meeting regularly throughout Britain and a vibrant Young Fabian section organising its own activities. Fabian publications, events and ideas therefore reach and influence a wider audience than those of any comparable think tank. The Society is unique among think tanks in being a thriving, democratically-constituted membership organisation, affiliated to the Labour Party but organisationally and editorially independent.

For over 120 years Fabians have been central to every important renewal and revision of left of centre thinking. The Fabian commitment to open and participatory debate is as important today as ever before as we explore the ideas, politics and policies which will define the next generation of progressive politics in Britain, Europe and around the world. Find out more at **www.fabian-society.org.uk**

Fabian Society
11 Dartmouth Street
London SW1H 9BN
www.fabian-society.org.uk

 Fabian ideas
Series editor: Jonathan Heawood

First published March 2005

ISBN 0 7163 0615 8
ISSN 1746-1146

British Library Cataloguing in Publication data.
A catalogue record for this book is available from the British Library.

Printed by Bell & Bain, Glasgow

The New Case for Europe

The crisis in British pro-Europeanism
– and how to overcome it

by
Roger Liddle

Contents

Preface

This pamphlet is written in a personal capacity. I was immensely privileged to work in 10 Downing Street as Tony Blair's European adviser for seven and a half years. I have since joined Peter Mandelson's 'cabinet' in the European Commission.

The views expressed here are however mine and mine alone. Any criticisms should be directed to me and no-one else.

My thanks are due to the Dartmouth Street Trust for funding the Fabian Society's Europe programme, which has made this publication possible. I would also like to thank my former colleague at Downing St, Sir Stephen Wall, who taught me more about Europe's workings than anyone else I know. I would like to dedicate this pamphlet to an older generation of Labour Europeans – the late Frank Pickstock, my mentor in Oxford labour politics in the 1970s and one time secretary of the Campaign for Democratic Socialism; Bill Rodgers, one time general secretary of the Fabians, for whom I worked in the Callaghan Government; and George Thomson, my father-in-law, Labour's first European Commissioner. They have been a lifetime's inspiration.

1 | A Referendum Labour Cannot Afford to Lose

L abour cannot afford to let the case for Europe go by default. The political costs of a referendum defeat would be incalculably high and possibly irrecoverable for this era of Labour government. Lose on Europe and we lose one of the crucial progressive platforms for the advance of modern social democracy.

It is no good hoping this difficult issue will somehow go away. It won't. In a historic triumph for democracy and peace in our continent, Europe has enlarged from 15 to 25 states; now this expanded EU needs to demonstrate that it can get its act together. The priorities are for Europe to revitalise its economic and social model and develop the capacity to be a more united and effective force for good in the world. Ratification of the Constitutional Treaty is important to the achievement of both.

Any club needs rules that govern those who choose to be its members. The rules for membership of the enlarged club now need to be settled for the foreseeable future.

The logic of ratification has grown steadily stronger, with December's decision on eventual membership for Turkey, and now the possibility of membership for Ukraine. In Euro-speak 'deepening' needs to accompany further 'widening'. While small groups can operate by consensus, an organisation of 30 members or more needs clear rules for decision making.

The French Socialist 'Yes' was a decisive moment, defeating those who argued that the Constitution does not offer a socialist enough vision of Europe's future. Against the odds, and with courageous leadership from Francois Hollande, the Socialist rank and file were persuaded at hundreds of packed meetings around France that in an insecure world, where Europeans are uncertain of America and fearful of globalisation, a stronger Europe makes obvious common sense.

The probability now is that the referenda in key Member States will be carried. In some cases this may require second thoughts, as in previous referenda in Denmark and Ireland. But there would be little chance of second thoughts for Britain.

A referendum defeat would leave a severely weakened Labour government stumbling along, torn between irreconcilable demands. On one side, the EU of 24 would want to press ahead. On the other, a British 'no' would hand the anti-Europeans in this country the platform they need to demand full renegotiation of British membership, with the aim of achieving the 'associate status' of their dreams.

Let there be no fudging of the magnitude of this divide. A referendum defeat cannot lead to a stable status quo. The British Eurosceptics are not 'sceptics' in the proper sense of being open to persuasion. The only compromise they will contemplate on Europe is frankly an extraordinary proposition. For them, it as an acceptable bargain for Britain to have continued access to the Single Market, which they admit is a vital national interest, on the basis that Britain would no longer play a part in the institutions that draw up and police the Single Market's rules.

On the other hand, for the EU 24, the Constitutional Treaty enshrines the transformation of Europe from a Single Market to a political Union, albeit one that is radically different from a federal United States of Europe and where the Member States retain a central role in legislation and policy. Our partners ruefully refer to this as *le constitution britannique*, but somehow we British pro-Europeans find it difficult to make the case.

The British pro-European case needs to be thoroughly refashioned. Europe cannot simply be explained to the British people as a free trade area vital to our prosperity. Pro-Europeans should no longer play down the political implications of the extensive framework of rules needed at European level in order to make the Single Market function fairly and be politically acceptable in other Member States. We cannot continue to peddle what first became the establishment consensus under Harold Macmillan in the late 1950s that there was 'no alternative' to British membership, with each step in European integration presented as both inevitable and constitutionally insignificant. The political significance of what has been at stake in building a new potential for political action beyond the nation state has to be *defended*, not underplayed. Pro-Europeans must acknowledge that the argument that Europe offered our economy a discipline that we were incapable of ourselves has lost its one time relevance, as Britain's relative economic performance has improved.

Instead, social democrats should make a bold progressive argument for Europe – something which Labour has never been prepared to do.

'If I list all the things that I have fought and written and argued for over more than 20 years – greater equality, the relief of poverty, more public spending, educational reform, housing policy, the improvement of the environment – I do not find that any of these will be decisively affected one way or another by the Common Market.'[1] With these words, Anthony Crosland, the iconic social democratic figure of his generation, elegantly washed his hands of the European issue in July 1971, as Labour faced a cataclysmic split over whether to oppose Edward Heath's terms of entry.

The central proposition of this pamphlet is that, in today's world, if you care like Crosland did, and I do, about equality, poverty, public spending, education, housing and the environment in Britain, not to mention social justice in the wider world, then you have no alternative but to be a committed pro-European. Labour governments in Britain cannot fulfil their full social democratic potential without a whole-hearted commitment to the EU.

Europe is essential to the success of the British progressive model for three big reasons. First, as a result of missing out on the full potential of the Single Market, which, to be fair, was only a theoretical vision in Crosland's time, British social democrats would sacrifice a significant dividend in economic growth and public spending that arises directly from our EU membership, and is in future potentially much bigger. The fact that we have performed better than Continental Europe for the last decade is irrelevant to this case. Outside Europe, Labour's ability to sustain high public spending and high-quality public services will be impaired.

Second, separated from the EU, Britain would cut its ties to a 'social market' model for economic development that embeds values and a framework of rules promoting social justice and environmental sustain-ability. In other words, it's not only growth potential we lose and the opportunity through additional public spending to distribute it in a fair way. We also cease to be bound into a distinctive European model for growth and we lose the political capacity to harness Europe's potential to mould global capitalism in a social democratic way. This is the modern alternative to the Keynesian, egalitarian model of nation state social democracy that Crosland espoused, but which is now unrealistic.

Third, outside the EU, Britain will in future be no more than an influ-ential, medium-sized power, in a world where China, India and Brazil are rapidly emerging as economic great powers. We may convince ourselves that a New Labour Britain represents a uniquely successful model of progressive advance, but outside the EU, we lose our capacity to multiply our influence, shape globalisation itself and be an effective force for good in the world. We would once again fall prey to the disease that afflicted Britain in the post war world – exaggerating our power and influence at the centre of Churchill's famous three concentric circles. We might still be a progressive beacon, as some would say Norway today is a shining example of a successful welfare society and progressive internationalism, but it would not be a beacon that shone a bright and powerful light across the oceans.

The essence of social democracy is a belief in the power of political action to provide greater opportunity and security for all. We are not pessimists who believe that the lot of our fellow human beings is either predetermined by nature, or shaped by market forces outside our control. In a world of increasing interdependence, we have at one and the same time to be conscious of the declining purchase of nation states on political phenomena beyond their reach and control, while supportive of international institutions that enable the power of political action to be re-asserted.

But the biggest plus for the European Union is that it is not a conventional international organisation. Most international organisations are chronically weak because they can only act by consensus between every sovereign country. The genius of Europe's founding fathers in the immediate post-war years was to recognise that this was an inadequate model for the integration they aimed for. The capacity for effective action would be strengthened the more sovereignty was 'pooled'. The essence of European governance is the balance between the supranational and the intergovernmental – but what makes Europe unique in terms of both effectiveness and legitimacy are those vital elements of supranationality – the Commission's right of initiative, the European Court's supremacy over national law, the directly elected Parliament and qualified majority voting in the Council of Ministers. What was devised to end centuries of bloody civil war in Europe turns out to be just what we need to advance our common European values in an age of globalisation.

The failure of successive British Governments to take on the anti-Europeans on this central argument (with some honourable exceptions, such as Tony Blair in his Cardiff speech in 2002) means that the public debate on Europe has advanced little in three decades. The referendum on the Constitutional Treaty will be make or break.

This is the modern progressive case for Europe. If we did not think that Europe itself really, really, mattered, then we would not waste any time debating a Constitution for it. But if, like me, you believe that wholehearted commitment to Europe is vital, then the battle for the Constitution is where it's at.

The worst argument for the Treaty is to focus on what it isn't, rather than what it is: 'Fear not, we have held back the Eurofederalist hordes that threaten our shores.' This feeds the suspicion that Europe is a conspiracy against our patriotic interests, and is hardly a convincing backcloth to the argument that a Britain fully committed to the European Union can play a leading role within it.

Progressives should instead argue for the Constitutional Treaty on its merits. To the running of Europe, it will bring greater clarity, greater effectiveness and greater democracy. The provisions of the Treaty, particularly its statement of values and objectives, and the incorporation of the Charter of Fundamental Rights, embed a progressive consensus that every progressive constituency – trade unionists, environmentalists, consumerists, those concerned for equal rights – should embrace with enthusiasm.

A more effective and democratic Europe will be stronger in addressing the challenges that Europe faces. Internally, the economic potential of Europe's Single Market is a cup half empty, rather than half full. Britain's own economic performance has been a triumph in the last eight years, but as we make up the ground from the Tory legacy of mismanagement and underperformance that we inherited, the deepening of economic integration in Europe will assume greater strategic importance in raising our own productivity and growth potential, and our continued capacity to finance the expansion of high quality public services.

Action at European level gives us the chance to strengthen the market opening that extends economic opportunities, whilst addressing the market failures in research, higher education, infrastructure and regional and social cohesion that hold back the development of a successful knowledge economy. The Constitutional Treaty offers us the flexibility to take part in this. It facilitates 'integration where necessary' while strengthening the ability of national Parliaments to force a rethink of new European legislation that is disproportionate and needlessly interfering.

British progressives should be aiming explicitly for a modern social democratic convergence between the best European standards of public service, environmental sustainability and social protection with our New Labour recognition of the need for enterprise and labour market flexibility. The Constitutional Treaty gives us a framework to work with our partners towards these political objectives.

Externally, a more effective Europe offers social democrats the best available chance of realising our goals in an interdependent world. A Constitutional Treaty cannot of itself make Europe more effective, but it does provide the machinery to ensure effectiveness, assuming the political will exists, especially among the larger Member States. Defence procurement can be streamlined; common military capabilities developed; military and civilian intervention in humanitarian crises coordinated; and a far more united front presented to the outside world through the creation of a European Foreign Minister and a stable Presidency of the European Council. All this can be added to the Union's already powerful position in trade and as the world's leading aid donor.

A realistic progressive goal for Europe is to build a more equal partnership between a more united and effective Europe and a genuinely internationalist United States, which will continue to be the ultimate guarantor of European and world security. But for Europe to be a credible provider of security in the 'arc of instability' that surrounds us – never mind aspire to a more equal transatlantic partnership – poses multiple challenges: to traditional German reluctance to contemplate the use of force, to French illusions of a multipolar world and to British conceptions of a special relationship with the United States. In particular, Europe will never be effective until Britain gives greater weight in its foreign policy to achieving a European consensus with its partners. Rather than threatening transatlanticism, as some right wing Americans argue, the Constitutional Treaty could help renew transatlanticism for a new age. However, Britain will have to adapt to a new conception of its role as a US-friendly partner within the European camp, rather than a transatlantic 'bridge'.

While it is possible to be pro-European in the modern world without being on the left, it is impossible to be on the progressive left without being a pro-European. And that is why the coming battle for Europe, and the referendum we cannot avoid, must be won.

2 | The Dangers of Complacency and Drift

L et the issue be put. Let the battle be joined.' With this brave flourish, Tony Blair concluded his Commons statement committing the government to a referendum on the European Constitution.[2] For the Prime Minister, this reversal of policy was a bold gamble. It would end a distracting argument about the government's allegedly undemocratic refusal to hold a referendum on the Constitution, and would pledge a historic plebiscite to resolve the long-standing ambivalence about Britain's place in Europe.

Yet the penumbra of public and party comment surrounding the announcement was less positive. True, the referendum announcement was widely praised at the time as a brilliant tactical manoeuvre. Labour had shot a menacing Tory fox. The announcement prevented the Conservatives from turning the 2004 European elections into a 'quasi referendum' on the Constitution, in place of the referendum proper that the Conservatives felt Tony Blair was certain to deny the British people. With Michael Howard and the Conservatives deprived of their planned battle cry, it was UKIP's crude withdrawalist message that attracted anti-Europeans. The electoral reverse for the Conservatives obscured a bad result for Labour and deflated any internal upheavals that might have followed.

Yet since the referendum announcement the trumpets of battle have sounded pretty mute. Will the serious battle for Europe ever be joined? Plenty have voiced their doubts. At the time that the referendum announcement was made, many assumed that the Constitution would never, in practice, be agreed. Perhaps the Labour government would 'up the ante', thicken its so-called 'red lines' and do its own little bit to make agreement less likely. Many of our partners assumed these were the British tactics. Some senior Ministers behaved as though they thought the same. It is to the great credit of the Prime Minister that he refused, point-blank, to go along. Tony Blair had a clear position. He stuck to it, he won it and, having won it, he agreed the Treaty at the next European Council.[3]

It then became received wisdom that the government would never be put to the test on the Constitution. It would be defeated in a referendum in some other Member State. So if Labour delayed, the whole embarrassing issue might simply go away. But at the time of writing, the idea of praying for an accident to get Labour out of a hole seems unrealistic.

There is a huge political danger for British pro-Europeans in thinking that the Treaty is certain to be derailed elsewhere. This will feed the assumption that a British rejection of the Constitutional Treaty would not really make much difference to anything – worse still, that it is an opportunity rather than a threat to our position in Europe, an opportunity for renegotiation, not an outcome that puts Britain on the slippery slope to withdrawal. This is precisely the line of argument the Tories would like to foster.

These reactions have a strong flavour of historical déjà vu. The British have consistently underestimated Europe and its capacity somehow to move forward. At the time of the Messina negotiations that led to the Treaty of Rome half a century ago, Rab Butler, the 'nearly man' of the Tory leadership in the 1950s, famously dismissed the discussions as 'some archaeological excavations in an old Sicilian town'. The unfortunate Board of Trade official, Russell Bretherton, who was sent to represent the British Government at Messina, announced his withdrawal from the talks with the infamous declaration that echoes through the decades of failed British policy towards Europe: 'Gentlemen, you are trying to negotiate something you will never be able to negotiate. But, if negotiated, it will not be ratified. And, if ratified, it will not work.'[4]

Nevertheless, it is easy to see why some Labour people might hope that the European Constitutional question will somehow just go away, despite the fact that the Party is now pretty united in its commitment to Britain's EU membership. The history of national referenda in other countries is of ticking time bombs under whichever political establishment goes in search of a 'Yes' vote. From the referendum on French regionalism that forced General de Gaulle's resignation in 1959 to the Danish rejection of the euro, which fatally weakened the legitimacy of Paol Nyrup Rasmussen's Social Democrat Government in Denmark in October 2000, the record warns of pitfalls ahead. Just look at the referendum in Britain on the North East Regional Assembly.

And the Europe issue poses unique dangers for the internal coherence of political parties, even when the evidence is overwhelming that, for voters, Europe comes fairly well down their list of priorities. Europe has been the vehicle for internal faction fighting in both our major political parties. It would be all too easy for some individuals to seek internal political advantage by claiming to be pro-Europe but against this Constitution (and argue that rejection of the Constitution is more likely to result eventually in a more effective and reformed European Union) – or while professing loyalty to Government policy, send off muted, or not so muted, signals of dissent. Even if one accepts the integrity of those who take this view, its advocacy opens the way to a lapse back into the kind of opportunism about Europe that so discredited the Labour Party in the past. According to Tony Benn's account, this reached up to the most senior figures in the Party:

> Went to talk to Harold. ... we also discussed the question of the Common Market. ... he made it absolutely clear that he is going to get off the hook by discovering that conditions for entry into Europe were not right.[5]

Sometime in the course of the last day or two, Jim Callaghan said to me that he took a strictly political view of the Common Market. He says he is sitting on the fence but he sees no reason at all why we, as a Party, shouldn't come out against the Common Market now and if we ever won an election, apply to join ourselves; indeed this would seem to him perfectly acceptable as a political manoeuvre.[6]

The British Referendum can only be won if, thirty years on, history does not repeat itself and the Party leadership stands united. So far unity has largely held, though Labour in office has done little to counter public or party lack of interest in matters European. The Prime Minister has made speeches setting out a stirring vision of Europe as a 'super-power, not a super state', as an expression of 'modern patriotism' and as 'our destiny'.[7] But across the government as a whole, Labour's practice of its European policy has been conceived through a narrow prism of national interest. Of course membership of the European Union is about the national interest. But it is not only that. For social democrats, it is a question of how politics can remain relevant in a world where globalisation is steadily eroding the capacity of nation states to build and sustain security and social justice.

Some may argue that the Constitution is a distraction. Why should a pro-European Labour Party use up its political capital and energies fighting for a Constitution that no one understands and few can see the relevance of! Surely, even pro Europeans can all breathe a sigh of relief if the whole thing fails at the ratification hurdle somewhere else? Yet the impulse that led the EU to embark on this process of institutional reform and Constitutional simplification would not disappear with a referendum 'No' in any country. The idea that Europe would live forever with the institutional 'status quo' established by the Nice Treaty of December 2000 may sound superficially plausible. Clever diplomatic minds in some quarters of the Foreign Office might even try to polish up the argument as a somewhat desperate face-saver of British EU membership, should the British referendum turn out wrong. But it is for the birds, and not going to happen.

In truth, were the British people to reject the Constitutional Treaty, it would not be because they regarded the concept of a Constitution for Europe as unacceptable in principle, or found on closer examination that the detail of this particular constitutional draft was flawed in some key respect or other. If they reject the Treaty, it will be because they are not convinced of the case for Europe.

Europe is no more popular with the British public now than it was in the early 1970s – or so the opinion polls tell us. A referendum will not be easy to win – and some pro-Europeans will hear that as an understatement. The specific polling on the Constitutional Treaty does not tell us much. The prevailing mood is ignorance, about which the public is refreshingly frank. More worrying from a pro-European point of view are increasingly negative attitudes towards Europe in general.

According to the Euro barometer poll that tracks public attitudes towards the European Union, more people now think Britain's EU membership a 'bad thing' than a 'good thing'.[8] That negative balance is a first in 20 years. In 1998, at the high point of the Blair honeymoon, the same figures registered two to one in favour.

In answer to the question, 'If you were told tomorrow that the EU had been scrapped', 45 per cent would be indifferent, 29 per cent very relieved and only 17 per cent very sorry. In Britain, 'withdrawalists' remain a minority, vociferous though they are. But the vulnerability of the pro-European position is demonstrated by the weakness with which sympathetic opinions are held. The pro-European base in Britain is tiny.

Yet pro-Europeans should not despair. At the time of the February 1974 General Election, fully 58 per cent believed that it was a mistake to join the Common Market, and only 28 per cent thought it the right thing to have done. A mere four months before the 1975 referendum, the figures were still 50-31 against. But in the June referendum itself, the vote was two to one in favour.

Admittedly, the 1975 victory was secured in more favourable circumstances than today's. Then there was a simple choice: stick with the status quo and stay in, or vote 'No' and face the uncertainties and dangers of withdrawal. Centre-ground opinion was united in support of EU membership, business was enthusiastic and the media far more supportive.

Now the pro European position is more difficult. Because 'core Europe's' economic performance is consistently presented as poor, British voters do not see how Europe today relates to their own day-to-day concerns for jobs, living standards and security. No one has set out a compelling vision as to how a fuller commitment to Europe will make life better for them – and this is particularly true for the losers from globalisation.

Public opinion will not be turned round without a massive fight, but the referendum battle can still be won. A vital essential is to hold out a vision of how Labour in government would want to use the Constitutional Treaty to promote our social democratic goals in Europe. This will require a shift in both presentation and substance: a more positive tone about Europe's pluses, and a greater willingness to spell out the policy areas where working together in Europe can be a help and not a hindrance.

The truth is that a referendum defeat would be an unmitigated political disaster for a third-term Labour government. Far from taking the troublesome issue of Europe off the political agenda, it would make the future of Britain's relations with Europe the abiding preoccupation of the remainder of Labour's third term. The risk would be that the issue of Europe would then move centre stage in party politics and completely overshadow the government's domestic achievements and ambitions. Those in Labour who regard Europe as a 'distraction' should remember that.

No one can foretell precisely the consequences of a British 'No', but it is impossible to believe that Britain on its own could simply block Europe's progress and enforce the Nice 'status quo' on our partners.

Our government would be desperate to find some acceptable basis for continued British membership. The likelihood also is that our partners would not be in a very sympathetic mood. In many of their eyes, the Constitutional Treaty is too British as it is – too much of a triumph of the stance that the Blair Government took in negotiations. In getting the Constitutional Treaty we have, we have almost exhausted our negotiating capital among the EU 24.

Of course we would have some cards to play. Most of our partners want Britain to be a committed member of the EU – including the French, where majority opinion strongly wanted Britain in the Euro and where as Dominique de Villepin put it, 'There can be no Europe without European Defence and no European Defence without Britain'.[9]

Should the EU 24 press ahead with the Constitution, there may be a halfway house on offer whereby we continue to gain the benefits of the Single Market without being full members of the European Union. That halfway house is the associate membership of the European Economic Area. Norway is a member already. It means we have to live by the Single Market rules all the others set and we no longer have a say in determining, in return for full access to the EU market and our trade not being discriminated against. So on financial services, the City of London would have to live with the rules that the EU sets without any British voice at the negotiating table to help shape them; similarly our car industry on safety and environmental rules and our telecoms industry on access to networks.

A solution on these lines must be a deeply unattractive proposition for a British government that was once ambitious to put Britain at the heart of Europe. Maybe it's a good bargain for Norway – but, without wishing to bang the nationalist drum, is it an acceptable deal for Great Britain?

This is where we would probably end up if a Conservative government were elected before the issue was resolved. It is a curious definition of bringing powers back from Brussels and 'regaining our national sovereignty'. The Conservatives might succeed as members of the EEA in negotiating Britain out of the Common Fisheries policy and the

Development Budget, as Michael Howard has pledged – but the EU 24 would undoubtedly insist that Britain continues to contribute to the cost of the EU Budget as a whole, because for the poorer members, the Structural and Cohesion Funds are the glue that binds the Single Market together. So we would have to accept a position as a net budget contributor, having lost the political clout to defend the British rebate.

The Conservatives also want to take Britain out of the Social Chapter. But many of our partners would be reluctant to offer us what they see as a free ride. Some already complain that Britain's flexible labour market and relatively low social minimum are an unfair competitive advantage. Rather, with Britain semi-detatching itself, the pressure would be the other way – to toughen up the social rules and harmonise standards to Britain's competitive disadvantage. A Conservative government would therefore be gearing itself up for a massive confrontation with the rest of Europe.

A referendum 'No' vote would be a huge advance for the forces of the Right, for whom withdrawal from Europe is a central obsession. Why – because they see Europe as getting in the way of their right-wing nirvana of rampant free-markets, aggressive deregulation, low taxes, privatised public services and a night watchman state. They see a vote against Europe as a re-assertion of an Englishness that is suspicious of foreigners and immigrants and tells the nations and regions of Britain where to get off.

In the Conservative Party and anti-European media, there are many closet withdrawalists who cynically regard the referendum as the first step in a two-stage process to detach Britain from Europe. A 'No' vote would give their morale and political position a huge boost. They simply would not let go – and their next demand would be that the Conservative Party pledge a referendum on withdrawal. Would Labour then go down the slippery slope of conceding a future referendum on withdrawal as a price of keeping Europe out of a General Election in 2009 or 2010 and securing a fourth-term General Election victory? I very much hope, for the Party's sake and for Britain's, that we will not be tempted.

Far better to concentrate on winning the referendum on the Constitution. Far better to use what would then be a devastating defeat for the Eurosceptics to strengthen our engagement with Europe. Far better to see victory in this first referendum as a way of unblocking the Euro issue and clearing the ground for an early campaign to take Britain into the euro when the economic conditions are right. In the present public mood, this may seem to some a flight of European fantasy. I see it, alongside the consolidation and advance of the domestic 'progressive consensus' that New Labour has created, as the third term fulfilment of the Blair premiership. Labour needs to gain the confidence to believe that, if we play it right, these prizes can be won. We would, in the process, have achieved an irreversible shift towards a more social-democratic Britain.

"

3 | Overcoming the Crisis in Pro-Europeanism

It will take more than simply a stronger political lead to win the case for Europe. We have to understand the plight of British pro-Europeanism and recognise that the old case for Europe no longer works. This isn't easy. What made me a strong pro-European was my first sight of the war cemeteries of Flanders. I shall never forget François Mitterrand's parting message to the European Parliament: *'Le nationalisme, c'est la guerre!'*[10]

Today, most Europeans take peace for granted. War between France and Germany is unthinkable. People enjoy unprecedented freedom to travel, study, work, holiday, buy homes and retire anywhere across the EU. Ernie Bevin's post war vision as Attlee's Foreign Secretary has come true: 'I want a world where the ordinary British citizen can go down to Victoria Station and buy a ticket to go anywhere he likes' – at any rate for the European Union – except that, today, it's likely to be Stansted or Luton, Ryanair or Easyjet, on a cheap air-fare that results from an EU liberalisation Directive that the European Commission initiated and pushed through – and of which the public knows little and cares less.

Yet, how many people attribute these extraordinary, historically unprecedented personal freedoms, and the peace and security which underpin them, to the institutions of the European Union? If people think of Brussels or even visit the EU capital, do they stand before the Berlaymont, the European Parliament building, or the Stalinist eyesore of the Justus Lipsius Building that houses the Council of Ministers, overcome by a rush of sentiment to pay tribute to the forefathers of the European Union and the achievements they have built? Most European citizens are either ignorant or indifferent. Even the historic miracle of enlargement to an EU of 25, which marks the unification of Europe after the end of the Cold War, has stirred very little emotion: where it has, this has more often been fear of immigration and competition for jobs.

The starting point for any case for Europe is simple. Invite people to look around. Bring home to them the sheer simple scale of what has been achieved: a united Europe of democracies living at peace with each other.

Of course, the sceptics who dominate sections of the UK media will ridicule this position. Many are locked in the crude 1940 imagery of Britain standing alone (ignoring the lessons that Winston Churchill himself drew from his wartime experience in calling for a United States of Europe from a balcony in Strasbourg). They behave as if they would prefer we were still fighting the Germans, even if the football pitch is a pale substitute for a real battlefield.

The more intelligent sceptics' position is that we can all enjoy Europe without having to bother with the European Union. But it is impossible to separate the present day Europe of Freedom from the European Union. The EU has proved itself time and time again an irresistible pole of attraction to people struggling to be free – to the anti-Fascists in the Iberian peninsula and Greece, to the new democracies of Central and Eastern Europe, to the people on the streets of Belgrade who brought down Milosevic and most recently to the people of Ukraine in overturning a fraudulent election rigged by a corrupt regime. British people who buy retirement homes in the Algarve, go on stag nights to Tallinn, or employ a Slovak nanny and a Polish builder all benefit directly from the EU's achievements.

But British pro-Europeans have never got on the same wavelength as this Europe of Freedom. 'Three million jobs at risk' often seems the limit of the British case for Europe. Indeed, the Britain in Europe campaign once claimed the figure was eight million, but then had to backtrack when the National Institute economists, on whose work the claim was allegedly based, refused to back it up. There is, of course, a strong relationship between jobs and prosperity on the one hand and Britain's assured membership of the European Single Market on the other. The Single Market, for all its failings, is the largest of its kind in the world: as a result of EU enlargement, it is larger in both population and wealth than the United States. But British pro-Europeans cannot win the argument for Europe by looking for some politically equivalent scare to the Tory Tax bombshell in the 1992 General Election – because the claim no longer seems credible and the economic context for Britain in which pro-Europeans have to make their case has completely changed in the last decade.

In recent years, the British case for Europe has been made largely in terms of economics and the national interest – another instance of the Thatcher effect. Few British politicians have been prepared to advance a broad political argument for European unity – not incidentally a charge that could fairly be levelled at the earlier Labour generations of Herbert Morrison in the 1950s, George Brown in the 1960s, Roy Jenkins in the 1970s or Neil Kinnock in the 1980s. Still less has Europe been presented as a great progressive opportunity. Instead, pro-Europeans have relied on a set of arguments first made by the Conservatives that economically Britain has no alternative. Where a broader argument has been made, it has been that Europe is the only option for a Britain in decline. This 'no alternative declinism' led British pro-Europeanism up a dangerous cul-de-sac, which became cruelly exposed in the disappointing and depressing aftermath of the 2003 Euro Assessment.

The impact of the old 'no alternative' argument has wilted and waned as Britain's relative economic decline has been partially reversed. The dangerous rut into which British pro-Europeanism has dug itself deep, needs to be explained further – and it is worth going over a bit of contemporary history just to understand how deep this rut is. For unless they fully understand their dilemma, British pro-Europeans will never be in a position to make a completely refashioned and compelling modern case.

From the 1950s, the core of the mainstream European argument was about reversing British national decline. Initially this was mainly an argument fashioned within the Conservative Party to persuade it to break with its Imperialist past. For Conservatives of the Macmillan and Heath persuasion, it was an essential part of an ill-specified modernisation strategy for Britain – even, as Wolfram Kaiser has argued, a substitute for facing up to more intractable vested interests at home.[11] The Common Market was seen as a more dynamic economic area, membership of which would magically raise Britain's growth rate. In the 1980s and 1990s, a new dimension was added. The commitment to Europe – in particular, the ERM and then the single currency – would provide a better guarantee of economic stability and low inflation. Europe was the alternative and the answer to Britain's chequered and often disastrous record of macro-economic management.

The high point of this position came at the turn of the 1990s. The coming of Europe's Single Market, heralded by the '1992' campaign, swung a wide swathe of elite and business opinion in favour of Europe. British membership of the ERM was supported by most of the Conservative Cabinet on the basis that it would provide the solid anti-inflationary anchor that the Conservatives' earlier experiments with monetary targets had failed to find. This was despite the long resistance of Prime Minister Thatcher herself, which was finally overcome by John Major as Chancellor of the Exchequer in September 1990.

Britain's forced ejection from the ERM on Black Wednesday in September 1992 can be seen in retrospect as a seismic calamity in the history of British pro-Europeanism.[12] It removed the commitment to Europe as the centrepiece of sound domestic policy. The Conservative pro-Europeans, who had been the most committed supporters of ERM membership, found it impossible to state the truth – that Britain had joined the ERM at the wrong time and at the wrong rate, and for the wrong reasons (to manipulate an interest-rate cut on the eve of Tory

Party Conference in 1990).[13] The Conservative anti-Europeans, on the other hand, seized on the collapse of their own government's policy as evidence that the British national interest and a European commitment could never be reconciled. They recruited to their side massed phalanxes of small business people who felt their livelihood had been sacrificed on an altar of high interest-rates dictated by Europe. They were confirmed in their view that Margaret Thatcher had been right all along and had been unfairly ejected from office in 1990 by a palace coup of Tory pro-Europeans. The Tory Party is still suffering from the near-fatal consequences of this emotional trauma.

But Britain's forced withdrawal from the ERM also threw Labour into confusion – a less visible confusion politically, but with long-term consequences for economic policy and Labour's commitment to the Euro and Europe. In the Shadow Cabinet, Neil Kinnock, John Smith and Gordon Brown had backed the ERM as a crucial symbol of Labour's commitment to financial stability and the slow rebuilding of public trust in the party's capacity for sound economic management. Labour adopted this policy, not primarily out of European conviction, but as a key stage in the Party's internal modernisation.[14]

Labour's brief but passionate love affair with the ERM was the outcome of a long debate within the Party about the feasibility of different economic strategies. The events surrounding the 1976 IMF crisis had exposed the limits of classic nation-state Keynesianism. The alternative economic strategy proposed heavy-handed interventionism in its place. But even when the force of the old left arguments for economic planning agreements began to fade, lingering attachments remained to ideas of export-led growth, stimulated by increased public borrowing and sustained by the 'freedom to devalue'. A pro-European variant to these nation state strategies for economic expansion was the concept of Euro-Keynesianism: the notion that co-ordinated reflation would lessen the external 'balance of payments constraint' on demand expansion by any single Member State, as all European economies would grow in parallel. Labour toyed with this key notion of the ERM, as the Shadow Cabinet was gradually brought round to a qualified acceptance of ERM membership. But the main attraction to the Party leadership was to put in place a framework of economic policy that gave an assurance of prudence and stability to both financial markets and voters. This approach was confirmed when Gordon Brown replaced Bryan Gould as Shadow Trade and Industry spokesman in the autumn of 1989.

Black Wednesday left Labour's modernisers without a clear economic framework of their own, unable to resurrect the ERM and hesitant about the even bigger commitment implied by the single currency. Hence, instead of Europe being the centrepiece of Labour policy through the ERM, there came about the highly qualified conditionality of the 'five tests' for membership of the single currency. In its place, Bank of England independence (though never fully spelt out prior to the 1997 election) assumed pride of place in New Labour thinking as the guarantee of external discipline against economic mismanagement.

Alongside these developments in policy, the British economy entered its longest period of continuous growth since records began. It was kick-started by the sharp devaluation of sterling that followed our exit from the ERM against a background of idle capacity. It avoided running into the inflationary buffers that had too swiftly halted previous expansions by the huge and permanent shock that ERM membership had delivered inflationary expectations, as Sir Alan Budd has argued.[15] This was arguably Europe's biggest single contribution to Britain's later success. Earnings growth remained manageable, despite increased tightening of the labour market – widely attributed to the long-term impact of the structural reforms of the 1980s. And it has been sustained beyond 1997 by the monetary and fiscal disciplines that New Labour imposed on itself, and the supply side reforms it pursued.

Not surprisingly, as Britain's relative economic performance has strengthened, the power of the old 'declinist' argument for Europe has weakened. In parallel, the attraction of the European model has itself declined. In the 1980s, Europe – in particular, the 'Rhineland model' –

was seen as the progenitor of a more successful and, for Social Democrats, more socially just form of capitalism than the raw crudities of Anglo-Saxon Thatcherism. Indeed, Germany and its Continental neighbours were seen as more successful precisely because they were more socially just. But, in the last decade, pro-Europeans have, catastrophically, allowed this argument to be completely turned around. Eurosceptics have secured widespread acceptance of two key propositions, first, that Britain is significantly outperforming the rest of Europe; and second, that this success is to a considerable extent due to the Anglo-Saxon flexibility that is now seen to characterise the British economy.

These claims are now central to British perceptions of Europe. In retrospect, supporters of early Euro entry had lost the argument before one word of the Treasury's voluminous Economic Assessment was written. In the absence of a clear 'knock down' argument in favour of membership, it was politically impossible to advance what would have been a strong but inevitably balanced case in the face of a popularly embedded prejudice that Britain would be mad to 'lock itself into a failing Euroland'. The idea that it might be advantageous to be fully part of a huge economic area, while at the same time enjoying the competitive advantage of greater flexibility than one's partners, never struck the decision makers as relevant.

Adverse perceptions of Europe's performance vis-à-vis Britain are pivotal to the debate about whether Britain should dig herself deeper into Europe, which is what acceptance of the Constitutional Treaty automatically implies to ordinary men and women. To win the referendum, pro Europeans must re-fashion this economic case for Europe. The economic message needs to be rid of its outdated 'no alternative', declinist connotations. Yes, Britain has enjoyed outstanding economic success since 1997. But only a Britain fully committed to Europe and its Single Market can maximise its future productivity and growth potential. And this will be more important in the years ahead than it has been in recent times, as the catch up effect of overcoming the Tory legacy of mismanagement and neglect wears off, and we become more dependent on opportunities in the wider European market to achieve our domestic economic goals.

More widely, pro Europeans must seize the opportunity offered by the debate on the Constitution to refashion their arguments. They have to make a broader political argument, of which economics forms a vital part – but only a part. This case must be bold and positive because it will be difficult to convince people that all they are being invited to endorse in a referendum is the codification of an unpopular European status quo. We must make a progressive case that escapes the outdated framework first set by the Macmillan Conservatives too long ago.

Critical to this progressive case is that Europe is as relevant to the challenges of the twenty-first century as it was to healing the divisions of two World Wars in the twentieth. If the EU's forefathers, two generations ago, had not invented the European Union as the means to end European wars, politicians of our generation would almost certainly be trying to establish something like the EU in order to tackle today's modern challenges – competing with the outside world in a new knowledge-based economy; making Europe's voice count in international financial architecture; providing leadership in the easing of Third World debt; greater integration in the defence industry and procurement; the challenge of crime, drugs and the environment. This is not my list. It was Tony Blair's, when he received the Charlemagne prize in 1999: 'In all these areas, I am suggesting Europe gets greater cohesion, strength and influence and uses it. In some areas, it will need greater integration. ... I say integrate where necessary, decentralise where possible.'[16]

How else can the nation states of Europe sensibly respond to the shifting power balances in the world and the rise of China and India as great powers but by building up Europe's collective strength? As Europe's share of world GDP inevitably declines, as billions in Asia work their way out of desperate poverty, does it not make compelling sense for us Europeans to pool our diminishing power and influence?

Take some more specific issues that have risen up the political agenda in the last ten years. How can we safeguard the free movement that Europeans now take for granted on our continent without working together at EU level to establish common rules and fair standards for the millions in the world outside who understandably want to migrate here? How can we succeed in the struggle to defeat terrorism if terrorists can escape justice by crossing our internal borders? How can we Europeans cope in future without a credible European Defence? How do we handle crises in our near abroad like the Balkans or North Africa without building up civilian and military capabilities for intervention?

The motivation for such action need not only be the Gladstonian moral impulse for internationalist intervention, which was lauded by progressive opinion during Kosovo and Afghanistan, but has become dangerously weakened after Iraq. Failing states can so easily result in hundreds of thousands of desperate refugees clamouring for entry at Europe's gates. Our own interests are directly at stake. We would be foolish to count on the Americans to solve our problems for us. Meanwhile, individual European nations lack the comprehensive range of capabilities for sustained military intervention.

These are powerful arguments – but they have been made only half-heartedly. Why – because they amount to an argument for 'more Europe'? It is difficult for any rising politician to stick their head above the parapet and argue for more Europe without the fear of early decapitation. That fear has to be overcome by collective leadership and example from the heavyweights of the Cabinet.

However, Europe's unpopularity in Britain is not due merely to lack of courageous leadership and outdated arguments. Pro-Europeans have to acknowledge that there is a problem of disconnection. This is not just a problem for Europe. It is a feature of public attitudes to all forms of politics and government today. It defies any single explanation. There is no doubt though that it reflects a declining public confidence, since the heyday of the post-1945 full employment welfare state, in the ability of politics to impact positively on people's daily lives. It also reflects the disengagement of those who see themselves as losing out from modernity and globalisation.

The problem of disconnection and disengagement is particularly acute in the case of the EU. Too many of Europe's citizens associate Brussels with unaccountable bureaucracy, undemocratic interference and an illegitimate waste of public money. These worries have a particular echo not just in Britain, but also across Europe – particularly in northern Member States and amongst some of the new members. On the Continent there is little of the outright Europhobia which grips so much of the British body politic, but there is a marked absence of Euroenthusiasm as well: in its place there is a well of uncertainty and suspicion.

There are two common explanations for this. The 'delivery' explanation is that the EU has lost its connection with the European public because it no longer delivers the dynamism, prosperity and jobs that were associated with the first successful decades of the Common Market. The 'legitimacy' explanation is that people are suspicious of what they see as a Brussels agenda for self-aggrandisement, which they perceive as largely outside the public's control, a classic case of something 'they' do to 'us'. There is not much point in debating which of these explanations is the more important: they are chicken and egg. Economic underperformance inevitably undermines Europe's legitimacy. Lack of legitimacy stands as a barrier to some of the measures necessary to tackle the underperformance.

A lot of Europe's problem is about economic performance, but not all. Were perceptions of the EU's economic performance to change, either as a result of internal structural reforms or some outside factor (an end to the United States 'miracle' or a crash in China, for instance), my guess is that the public concerns would lessen, but still be significant. First, the Single Market is economically vital – but the rules necessary to bring it together are intrusive. On the Government's own admission, 50 per cent of the legislation affecting business is now made in Brussels. Second, the issues raised by the pooling of sovereignty in order to make the Euro a success are of a different political order from those concerning the Single Market. This is not an argument against the Euro, which I strongly support, only an argument that the political and constitutional issues cannot be brushed aside as irrelevant or minor. Third, as the case for 'more Europe' extends into areas that have traditionally gone to the heart of the nation state, like criminal justice, immigration, foreign policy and defence, the debate about legitimacy and accountability is bound to intensify.

For all these reasons, the institutional debate on Europe's Constitutional Treaty is not an unnecessary distraction. Nerd-like though the details of this debate may be, its outcome is vital to whether Europe can gain the legitimacy and effectiveness to fulfil its potential.

"

4 | The Progressive Case for the Constitution

Constitutions are, by their nature, dry affairs. Few Labour Party members aspire to be the barrack-room lawyer who knows the rule book backwards and delights in points of order. Most have never read the rule book but are no less committed for that. Yet constitutions matter. They set the rules members all abide by.

The common sense argument for the Constitutional Treaty is that the EU needs rules. No one can be a member of a club, or play a game, if they are not prepared to sign up for its rules. A theoretical distinction can be drawn between 'constitutive' rules and 'regulatory' rules. 'Constitutive' rules shape the rules of the game: without the existence of such rules, there cannot be a game like chess. 'Regulatory' rules shape the game's outcomes: for example, the rules of distributive justice that social democrats care about.

The Constitutional Treaty sets the constitutive rules for the co-operative relationship between EU members. If there were no rules, the EU could not exist.[17] The determined opponents of the Constitutional Treaty in Britain just don't get this basic point. For them, it is states which have constitutions, and they don't want the European Union to be a state. In their eyes, a constitution suddenly gives the European Union a special character it never had before – and there is no doubt that this point has some resonance with the public. A Constitution seems very big, very definitive and very irreversible.

Supporters of the Constitution have to explain that the means for its adoption is a Treaty between sovereign Member States, just like every Treaty that preceded it – and any new Treaty in future that may succeed it. These past Treaties include the Single European Act and the Maastricht Treaty. Both had profound consequences for Britain's relations with Europe, containing major new 'chapters' extending EU competence. But past Conservative Governments signed and pushed them through to Parliamentary ratification without a referendum. Consistency has never been a strong point in party politics when it comes to Europe. These points will be well on display in the partisan cut and thrust of the referendum campaign itself.

However, for social democrats, this Constitutional Treaty has a significance beyond the fact that it codifies a set of rules necessary for membership of the club:

> **First**, it embeds social democratic values.
>
> **Second**, it clarifies the EU's powers without putting Europe in a neoliberal straightjacket.
>
> **Third**, it enables 'more Europe' where co-operation is needed, while providing new guarantees against Brussels centralisation.
>
> **Fourth**, it makes Europe's institutions more effective and more accountable, helping to close Europe's 'delivery deficit' and making the governance of Europe more accountable to elected politicians and ordinary citizens.
>
> **Fifth**, it ends the spectre of a 'European Superstate' by defining the new consensus on European co-operation and integration.

1. The Treaty embeds social democratic values

The Constitutional Treaty doesn't pre-determine outcomes, but creates a 'values context' for those outcomes – one which social democrats should embrace with enthusiasm but which causes deep tremors on the right. We tend to think that the right is obsessive about Europe because it is obsessive about national sovereignty. But imagine for a moment that by some miracle of geography, the British Isles could be transported across the Atlantic and located twenty miles off the Maryland coast. Would the right be so vociferous in arguing on national sovereignty grounds that Britain should never become the 51st State of the USA? No. It is what Europe stands for with which the Right has its biggest problem.

The Constitutional Treaty marks the completion of a long transition from the free market Europe of the Treaty of Rome in the 1950s to the European Union of today: a political Europe, and a co-operative entity based on shared values, not the solely free-market Europe that made so many trade unionists and Labour Party members originally suspicious of British membership. This is clear from the opening clauses of the Constitution and is underwritten in the horizontal social clauses in Part Three. (**See Box 4.1**)

More controversially, the Charter of Rights, proclaimed at the Nice European Council in December 2000, becomes the legally binding Part Two of the Constitution. The Charter contains a range of economic and social principles, in addition to the political and human rights that were a feature of the ECHR and are now incorporated in UK domestic law through Labour's Human Rights Act.

These principles range widely across what we would think of a progressive social agenda including the entitlement to social security benefits and social services and the right to social and housing assistance to ensure a decent existence for all those who lack sufficient resources. They also include certain 'decency' provisions for employment: the right to protection against unjustified dismissal; the right to working conditions that respect health, safety and dignity; the right to limitation of maximum working hours, to daily and weekly rest periods and to an annual period of paid leave; the protection of young people at work; the right to paid maternity leave and to parental leave.

The principle of a legally binding Charter of Rights has been one of the most contentious issues in the UK. But should it be so controversial? A generation ago, the notion of a set of justiciable rights that might chal-

---

Box 4.1: A social democrat's Constitution
• Article Two states that 'the Union is founded on the values of respect for human dignity, liberty, democracy, equality, the rule of law and respect for human rights'.
• Article Three goes on: 'the Union shall work for sustainable development based on balanced economic growth and price stability, a highly competitive social market economy, aiming at full employment and social progress. It shall combat social exclusion and discrimination, and shall promote social justice and protection, equality between men and women, solidarity between the generations and protection of the rights of the child. It shall promote economic, social and territorial cohesion and solidarity among Member States'.
• Under the general provisions of Part Three, the Constitution states: 'in all the activities referred to in this part, the Union shall aim to eliminate inequalities, and to promote equality between men and women'. And it adds, for the first time, that 'in defining and implementing the policies and actions referred to in this Part (i.e., all its internal policies), the Union shall take into account requirements linked to the promotion of a high level of employment, the guarantee of adequate social protection, the fight against social exclusion, and a high level of education, training and the protection of human health'. It also adds for the first time: 'the Union shall aim to combat discrimination based on sex, racial or ethnic origin, religion or belief, disability, age or sexual orientation'.

---

lenge the doctrine of Parliamentry sovereignty was anathema to many on the Left. But the experience of Thatcherism and the campaigning success of bodies like Charter 88 overcame that inhibition. Isn't it in keeping with this change of mood that citizens should have their basic rights guaranteed in a Constitutional Treaty that lays down the rules for EU governance? Giving rights to citizens against abuses of political or bureaucratic power might even help counter the present disengagement with politics, and overcome mistrust of politicians. (**See Box 4.2**)

The Labour government held back from making this case for the Charter, fearing that it could be seen as a 'Trojan horse' for reversing the Thatcherite industrial relations settlement. Indeed, the government succeeded in securing amendments in the final stages of the IGC negotiations which ensure that the European Courts will not have the legal right to override national laws for which national Parliaments are responsible. This has caused hurt to the trade unions, with accusations that the government has 'neutered' the Charter.

But if we pause to think, the Government's position must be right. No EU Treaty makes the right to strike an EU competence – the social clauses of the existing treaties specifically exclude this. For once this exclusion is not because of the British. Germany is highly protective of its co-determination laws, and prohibits public service workers from going on strike. Whether these should remain is a question for the

---

Box 4.2: The Charter embraces...

• the right of Freedom of Assembly and Association, 'which includes the right of everyone to form and to join trade unions for the protection of his or her interests';

• workers' rights to Information and Consultation (within Article II-27) which states 'workers or their representatives must, at the appropriate levels, be guaranteed information in good time in the cases and under the conditions provided for by Union law and national laws and practices';

• and the right of Collective Bargaining and Action (Article II-28), which states: 'workers and employers, or their respective organisations, have, in accordance with Union law and national laws and practices, the right to negotiate and conclude collective agreements at the appropriate levels and, in cases of conflicts of interests, to take collective action to defend their interests, including strike action'.

German voter and the German Parliament. So should it be in Britain. To permit the European Court to overturn national laws on the basis of a constructive legal interpretation of a legally binding EU Charter would be undemocratic.

However, the Charter is not neutered as it affects the exercise of EU competence. It gives individuals, trade unions and other civil society groups a legal right to go to court if they believe their fundamental rights are being breached in acts for which the European Union is responsible, or where Member States are acting on the Union's behalf. For example, if some element of the proposed new Services Directive were established as threatening the principle of equal access to public services, or the rights of workers to health and safety protection, then the Charter could be used to defend those rights. It is properly an EU Charter relevant to EU competences, and not for national decisions outside EU competence. As such, it represents a large gain for fundamental rights.

Nothing in the Constitution weakens the position of the trade unions – indeed, it fully recognises the position of the trade unions in society. Under Article 47 of Part One: 'the European Union recognises and promotes the role of the social partners at Union level, taking into account the diversity of national systems; it shall facilitate dialogue between the social partners, respecting their autonomy'. No British Act of Parliament similarly enshrines the principle of social partnership. Nothing in the Constitution rolls back Social Europe and the Labour government's decision in 1997 to sign up for the Social Chapter, which has already helped rebalance the post-Thatcherite settlement. But the ideological opponents of the Constitutional Treaty would use the platform of a British 'No' vote to achieve a Social Charter opt-out.

These values and rights set a framework for policy and define a standard against which proposals for future action can be judged. They do not predetermine policy outcomes or rule out a range of political choices. But they set limits on what the EU counts as politically possible, and set some basic obligations of membership for Member States. This is particularly important to Britain where the values of the British people have always been on the centre-left, but the polarisation of our political system has often led to sharp ideological u-turns in public policy.

The British people should feel at home in Europe because the Constitution's values are British values too. The political challenge that the Constitution poses is to the hard right: those who dabble with racist populism or define their paradise as a socially conservative minimal state with free markets unconstrained by considerations of social justice. A right-wing populist government would still have the sovereignty to act as they wished – but ultimately they could not pursue their ideologies as members of the EU. People like John Redwood might rejoice in that – but they would have to win the case for withdrawal from Europe first. That would become a high hurdle once the referendum on the Constitution is won. So the EU and its Constitution can play an important role in reinforcing a progressive social consensus.

2. The Treaty clarifies EU powers, without putting Europe in a neo-liberal straightjacket

There has been much intellectual sneering at the Constitution's length (over 300 pages), and criticism of its inelegance by contrast with the short simple prose of the United States Founding Fathers. This criticism is unfair. Part One of the Constitution is well written and of readable length. It summarises what the EU is, what it exists to do, what its powers are and how decisions are made through the careful balance of powers between its various institutions. This is a successful exercise in 'simplification', part of the mandate that the European Council gave the Convention charged with producing the draft.[18] An intelligent sixth-former in search of a clear explanation of European governance could do a lot worse than read Part One, though there would, no doubt, be those in Britain who would condemn 'bringing political propaganda into the classroom'.

Another common criticism – that the Constitution represents a missed opportunity to 'reform Europe' – is also wide of the mark. This is principally levelled at Part Three of the Constitution, which makes up the bulk of the text and represents a consolidation of 50 years of painstaking compromise between the Member States in defining the separate policies of the Union and the rules for their implementation. The complexity reflects the true nature of the Union: it is not a simple Federation taking decisions on a majority basis, but a unique political entity whose sovereign Member States have conferred it specific powers. A call for greater simplicity means, in practice, less respect for national idiosyncrasies, not an outcome that Eurosceptic critics would welcome.

Critics also argue that the drafters failed to seize the chance to re-define the relationship between the Union and the Nation State. In her recent Fabian pamphlet, Gisela Stuart describes herself as pro-European but bemoans the lack of a thorough rethink.[19] Implicit in many such criticisms is a belief that European powers have become too wide as a result of the supposed instincts of a 'Brussels elite' to extend European competences wherever it can, as a result of its own bureaucratic momentum.

Should the Constitution have defined EU competences more rigidly than it does, and returned powers to the Member States? At the outset of the Convention, many Germans from Länder governments – mainly but not solely from the Right – favoured the concept of a strict Competence Catalogue. The Convention responded by creating three categories of competence: exclusive, shared and supplementing. The Union's 'exclusive' competences (where only Europe can make laws and exert power in the field of policy) are strictly limited – in effect to trade, cross-border competition, fisheries and monetary policy (for members in the euro-zone). The very narrow limitations of these exclusive competences hardly suggest a 'centralised superstate'.

'Shared' competences range over a wider field. Only in cases where the Union chooses to legislate can it override national laws. Whether these 'shared' competences should have been defined more narrowly comes down to questions of political preference. A pure free market liberal would strictly limit the EU's internal role to market liberalisation. But there is more to life than the market. It could be argued that the EU should confine itself to market liberalisation, leaving Member States and regions free to make market interventions to correct for market failures. But there is an obvious problem: one person's legitimate intervention is another person's unfair distortion.

Take the current debate about the future of the Structural Funds. Britain is pressing to phase out the EU's regional funds for the prosperous members of the old EU 15 and to concentrate the Structural Funds on transfers to the much poorer new Members, in order to keep the EU Budget to 1 per cent of GDP. This would 'renationalise' regional policy funding in the richer member states. But there would inevitably be complaints about subsidies to industry, and intense pressure to define the State Aid rules more restrictively with new EU rules to govern Member State regional policies. If, as I believe, we should combine the vigorous pursuit of open markets with a strong cohesion policy then there is a social democratic argument of principle for maintaining the present scope of the Structural Funds. A similar argument applies to EU social policy. This isn't to say that every piece of social harmonisation legislation that comes out of the Commission has merit. It doesn't. But it is very difficult for a social democrat to argue that the EU should not have some shared competence in social and labour market questions.

The absence of a rigid 'Catalogue of Competences' from the Constitution is a strength, not a weakness. Social democrats should beware of the example of the United States, where until the New Deal, American conservatives used the hierarchy of competences in the US Constitution to limit federal power and constrain the federal government's efforts to pursue social solidarity and social justice. It is a good thing that the EU has chosen to give itself a more flexible rule book. No one can foretell the future with perfection. Who would have thought, ten years ago, that the battle against cross-border terrorism would have become a major EU preoccupation? The Constitution's flexibility over competences creates the capacity for more Europe in future – but only where the case for more Europe can be intellectually established and politically won.

3. The Treaty enables 'More Europe' where it is needed – but with new safeguards against more Brussels centralisation

The Constitutional Treaty does not involve a radical, formal extension of EU powers. It launches no new 'grand projet' of the ambition of the single currency. But it increases the chances that the EU's existing formal powers will be exercised more effectively.

European Foreign Policy has been built up gradually. The Maastricht Treaty first formalised the EU's ambitions to establish a Common Foreign and Security Policy and its aspiration for Common Defence. The Amsterdam Treaty led to the appointment of the EU's first external High Representative, Javier Solana, while European Defence was launched as a bilateral UK-French initiative at the 1998 St Malo Summit and translated into operational EU texts at successive European Councils. The Constitutional Treaty now pulls all this previous activity together in a single place. These new institutional arrangements, painstakingly negotiated with the full participation of the British Government, will enhance the credibility of a common European Foreign Policy, as long as the basic consensus exists between Member States to make them work. (**See Box 4.3**)

Similarly in Justice and Home Affairs, formally the Treaty merely develops the political decisions taken previously in the Maastricht and Amsterdam Treaties. Because most decisions in the fields of justice and home affairs will now be taken by qualified majority, this will facilitate effective European action on questions of immigration, asylum and cross-border crime.[20]

In other areas, the Constitution offers Europe new flexibility to establish 'core groups' in areas where not all Member States are ready to act, and permits Member States participating in these 'core groups' to move ahead by majority decision. The usual defeatist assumption is that

---

Box 4.3: Europe's strengthened role in foreign policy and defence

• A single 'European Foreign Minister' replaces the present confusing split of functions between the Council of Foreign Ministers' High Representative (Javier Solana) and the External Relations Commission (formerly Chris Patten, now Benita Ferraro-Wallner). The new Foreign Minister both sits in the Commission and chairs the Council of Foreign Ministers on a permanent basis. This gives the holder of this new post a considerable degree of authority.

• A new European External Action service will bring together the staff of the Council, the Commission's external representations and secondees from the Member States, to provide the Foreign Minister, Council and Commission with high quality advice and a strengthened capability for diplomatic intervention.

• The new Treaty codifies the respective security roles of the EU and NATO, and political agreement has been reached accompanying it on how the build up of an EU Military Staff will be compatible with NATO.

• A new Agency is set up to streamline defence procurement.

• New provisions are included in the Treaty to enable 'core groups' to develop common military capabilities that they cannot afford on their own.

• The Union gains 'single legal personality' which makes it easier for Europe to sign international Treaties on behalf of Member States.

Britain would never be part of these 'inner cores' and will never want to work more closely with our partners. This is patent nonsense. In defence, Britain has led in establishing the new European Capabilities Agency.[21] In other areas, like public funding of research, we might want to develop common programmes with those EU partners who are prepared to commit the necessary resources.

While enabling the EU to act effectively, the Treaty provides new means to prevent any uncontrolled escalator of Brussels centralisation.

For the first time in an EU Treaty, the Constitution makes clear that, if a competence is not listed as an EU competence, then the Member States have chosen not to confer it on the EU. Europe has no powers by right, only those which Member States choose to confer. Other questions remain of sole national competence. The scope of national politics remains very wide. Because they have not been 'conferred' on the EU, the structure and funding of the NHS, the design of the school curriculum and the organisation of the education system, the scope and level of social security benefits, pensions policy, the degree of devolution to local government and regional bodies, questions of policing and the organisation of the criminal justice system – to quote just a few examples – all remain questions entirely for Member States' sovereign decision.

The Constitution also introduces important new rights for national Parliaments over new EU legislation. They will be involved more closely, and earlier, in the process of European legislation than ever before. When the Commission makes any initial legislative proposal, national Parliaments gain a new right to decide whether they think this is an appropriate piece of legislation to propose at European level. If a third of national Parliaments in the EU object, the Commission is required to think again. Critics claim this is a toothless provision. But national parliaments have a strong self-interest in being stern guardians against any overweening Brussels centralisation. In political reality, if national Parliaments across the Union mobilise opposition, the Commission will have no alternative but to back down.

My concern is rather that the new provision could prove toothless in the UK. Will the British Parliament ever get around to exercising its new constitutional rights over European legislation in a proper way? Its current scrutiny of European business does not fill one with confidence. The House of Lords, with its high-quality analysis of European issues, does a much better job than the Commons. But, as so often, the real obstacle to Parliamentary scrutiny is the executive's grip on the Commons. The Whips have traditionally resisted any arrangement that gets in the way of Ministers (and their officials) deciding what they want, and when they want it, in Brussels. This weakness lies in British democracy, not an EU 'democratic deficit'.

Parliaments in other Member States exert more effective control over how their Ministers act in Europe. In Finland, the Cabinet's European committee meets every Friday morning to decide EU policy for the coming week and then debates its decisions with the powerful Europe Committee of the Finnish Parliament on Friday afternoons. This does not depend on ratification of the Constitutional Treaty. Britain could copy the Finnish example straight away, though MPs' enthusiasm for doing this on a Friday might be limited! The Constitution offers new opportunities to strengthen democratic scrutiny. To exercise these powers effectively, the UK parliament will need to become quicker off the mark, more independent of the executive, better informed about Europe, and more engaged with Parliamentarians in other Member States.

4. The Treaty makes Europe's institutions more effective and more accountable

At the heart of the case for the Treaty is that it contains the necessary institutional reforms to enable an enlarged Europe to deliver. The enlarged European Union must close the 'delivery deficit' by building a more effective and transparent partnership between the three most important EU institutions: Commission, Council and Parliament. The Constitution's proposals recognise that none of these institutions would, unreformed, be effective in the enlarged Europe. But only by increasing accountability and transparency at the same time will Europe enhance its legitimacy in the eyes of its citizens.

The realities of interdependence drive member states to co-operate even more closely in areas that were once seen as exclusively within the domain of national sovereignty. As Europe enters these 'sacred gardens' of national sovereignty, the question of clear political accountability and transparency must be tackled. Otherwise the brakes will be applied to further European integration. Even where 'more Europe' makes sense, there will be a reluctance to pool sovereignty over any new policy domains in a political system that some see as untransparent, inefficient, and unable to deliver. Large sections of the British governing class are effectively in this camp.

Pro-Europeans should acknowledge that there is a problem of bureaucratic accountability in the EU, though it is a more complex issue than the standard attacks on 'Brussels' or the Commission recognise. The Commission proposes and the Member States dispose – but governments do this largely through the national Member State officials who do the groundwork for periodic meetings of Councils of Ministers. This can result in a bureaucratic Europe where real power has lain in the hands of Commission and Member State officials, political priorities are obscure and decision-making less than transparent. This bureaucrats' Europe has grown in power and prominence, undermining Europe's legitimacy. A disconnection has emerged between the political level – the Europe of *grand projets* such as the Single Market, Social Europe, the single currency and enlargement – and the engine room of European decision making. This disconnection has become more acute as the grandest European project of all – growth, prosperity and employment for all Europe's citizens – has faltered and Europe's efforts to reverse that faltering through 'Lisbon' have so far produced little result.

Pro-Europeans have responded to Europe's problems of legitimacy and efficiency in different ways. Tony Blair believes that public support for further integration can be sustained by demonstrating to the European public that their national governments are fully in charge of the process, ultimately through the democratically elected Heads of Government assembled in the European Council. To a remarkable extent, well understood on the Continent but totally underappreciated in Britain, the Constitutional Treaty represents a triumph of this Blairite view.

But Blair's concern is also that the European institutions can work effectively in a Europe of 25 or more, and that the widening of Europe must not prevent 'deepening' where Europe should act together in future. He has said that 'people worry that the Council and Commission may end up in opposition to each other. The real worry is that both are going to face far greater strain on their efficacy because of the sheer number of members. There are distinct and vital roles for both and both need strengthening', he has said. 'The objective should be a Europe that is strong effective and democratic. This requires a strengthening of Europe at every level'.[22] (See Boxes 4.4-4.6)

The importance of the full range of the Constitution's reforms is often lost in a British debate where the institutional debate is viewed through a false prism. More power to the Commission and Parliament is seen as a triumph for supranationalism: more power to the Council as a triumph for intergovernmentalism and all that Britain should want. But

---

Box 4.4: The European Commission

Its role: The Commission – Europe's executive – is more than a civil service and less than a government. It has the power of initiative, but mostly not of decision. It manages EU spending programmes, has an independent regulatory role on questions of State Aid and competition, and it negotiates trade agreements on behalf of Member States.

The problem: The Commission is supposed to act exclusively in the European interest. But the growth in EU members has made the institution unwieldy. The risk is that Commissioners see themselves as representative of their Member State, not defenders of the Common European interest.

Proposed reforms: The European Commission will be smaller. This will ensure that each Commissioner has a proper job to and enable the Commission to set more coherent priorities. As only two thirds of Member States will have Commissioners at any one time, Commissioners will be more likely to represent the European interest rather than that of their Member State.

The New Case for Europe

Box 4.5: The Council of Ministers and European Council

Its role: The Council of Ministers is drawn from all Member States and meets periodically in different formations of particular national Ministers. Foreign and Finance Ministers meet monthly. Heads of Government meet four times a year in the European Council. The Council of Ministers has to approve all legislation (by unanimity or qualified majority, according to subject) and decide on common policies. The Council is supported at official level by a myriad of working groups made up of national officials, of which COREPER, the Permanent Representatives' Committee in Brussels, is the apex.

The problem: The Council works – after a fashion. The system is dominated by unelected officials, not Ministers. Member state officials in Council working groups tend to pursue the interests of their own department, rather than working to a cohesive set of European priorities, sometimes pushing regulations throughout Europe that they cannot get through to their own national government.

Proposed reforms: The Council of Ministers will gain stronger political leadership. The absurdity of the six-monthly rotating Presidency will be abolished. The European Council will have its own full time President, serving for a two-and-a-half-year term, renewable once, and Team Presidencies will chair the Council of Ministers. Strong integrationists criticise the fact that unanimity will still be required in reserved areas of special national sensitivity – all tax decisions, big foreign policy decisions, anything to do with defence, future Treaty change and the question of who pays what amount to the EU budget. This list of course emphasises Britain's success in preserving our 'red lines', though other Member States were equally exercised about some of these issues. On other issues, the threshold for a qualified majority – 55 per cent of Member States and 65 per cent of the EU population – will be easier to obtain than under the complicated voting formulae of the Nice Treaty. Decisions will be made more speedily and the quality of legislation should improve.

44

Box 4.6: The European Parliament

Its role: The European Parliament is the directly elected representative body of all Europe's citizens. The number of MEPs for each country reflects population, but the smaller states are overrepresented. Its powers have increased over the last decade, and the Parliament's support is necessary to elect the Commission President and his team of Commissioners. The Parliament's greatest power is of 'co-decision' with the Council over many areas of legislation and the budget, with a formal 'conciliation' procedure where Council and Parliament disagree.

The problem: Many MEPs work extremely hard, and in their own areas of specialist interest can have a far bigger say over legislation than any Westminster backbencher could dream of. But the collective standing of the Parliament remains weak and the profile of its members is still low, despite its recent triumph in the Buttiglione affair in forcing changes in the membership of the Barroso Commission.

Proposed reforms: Co-decision with the European Parliament will apply in virtually all areas of legislation and decision-making. European Parliament assent will have to be attained alongside that of the Council for most things Europe does. Co-decision is particularly significant on the question of the distribution of the European budget, and agriculture policy. Up to now, the Parliament's toothless Agriculture Committee has been no more than a ramp for farmers' interests. As the Parliament gains real power over how much of the European budget should be spent on agriculture, the hope must be that the collective voice of all EP members will give due weight to the 95 per cent of EU population who are not farmers and wish to see the 40 per cent of the EU Budget now devoted to agriculture spent on more socially productive purposes. This opens up a crucial political opportunity at European level for social democrats.

the European Union is, and always has been, a complex hybrid of inter-governmentalism and supranationalism.

The Blair government certainly advocates a vision of Europe where the Council sets the Union's broad strategy and policy objectives; so have most Continental governments for certainly the last quarter century. What could all the emphasis on the historical importance of the 'Franco-German motor' mean if not a leadership role for the Member States exercised through the Council? The democratic legitimacy of Europe has derived from the impetus given to the European project by its Member States, and a Britain fully committed to Europe could have played just as major a leading role as France and Germany have in the past. But successive British Governments have failed to explain fully the institutional tools which are essential to making Europe work. In essence, the Single Market rests on a supranational triad: a strong Commission to initiate legislation and enforce competition; majority voting in the Council of Ministers to break the power of Member States vested interests to hold up legislation; and an authoritative European Court to uphold European law.

The reforms which make Europe more effective also make Europe more transparent. The key role of the European Council in deciding strategy will be highlighted by the visibility of the permanent President. Both the President of the European Council and the new European Foreign Minister will be major actors in European politics Their high profile existence will increase the public accountability of what they do.

Other reforms in the Constitutional Treaty will also increase account-ability. Every formation of the Council of Ministers will vote in public on legislation. No longer will national Ministers be able to get away with blaming legislation on 'Brussels' that they themselves voted through the Council. The European Parliament is at long last, coming of age. The very existence of the Constitutional Treaty, regardless of the institutional reforms it contains, marks a critical stage in the transition from a bureaucratic Europe to a more political Europe. The muscle that the European Parliament has shown in rejecting the first Barroso

Commission owes nothing to the detailed provisions of the Constitutional Treaty. It owes a lot, however, to the debate about Europe's legitimacy that the constitutional discussion has engendered. With the Parliament's new, widened powers, the public and the media should, at last, sit up and take notice.

Social democrats should support the Constitutional Treaty because it makes this European System more effective, and improves the transparency and accountability of the EU. But increased political control and accountability depends on what member states do at national level too. A major step in improving accountability between Brussels and Westminster would be the appointment of a senior Cabinet Minister for Europe to co-ordinate all European business – again, something that should flow from ratification, but is not mandated by it. He or she would spend a couple of days a week in Brussels attending the Council of Ministers, and would answer directly to the Commons for their actions. This new post would establish visibly and clearly that the Council of Ministers takes the key decisions in Brussels – and that the Minister representing Britain is directly accountable back home. The Foreign Office will resist this diminution of its institutional power. But this is a classic example of vested interest standing in the way of a reforming Government. We don't need the Constitution to adopt this practice. But a Labour government has within its power to strengthen the greater accountability to national Parliaments that the Constitution facilitates.

5. The Constitutional Treaty sets out the new consensus on European co-operation and integration – ending the spectre of a 'European Superstate'

Fears that the European Union will become too powerful as a result of the Constitutional Treaty are unfounded. The Treaty sets out the new European consensus on how members co-operate within the EU – a settlement which British and European social democrats should support. The Constitutional Treaty is a long way from the old Federalists' dream of a United States of Europe.

In 1945, there was logic in being a Federalist. If Europe was to avoid a repeat of its dreadful history, then a dramatic reshaping of the Westphalian order of state sovereignty, and nineteenth-century nationalism, seemed necessary. The basic Federalist idea of submerging discredited nationalism in a new form of multi-national, multi-tiered governance, in which citizens would develop a common identity and interests as Europeans, won partial converts in surprising quarters. In the desperate straits of 1940, Winston Churchill had proposed a permanent Union of Britain and France and, post-1945, it was his call, from a balcony in Strasbourg, for Franco-German reconciliation in a 'United States of Europe' that gave the Federalist movement its impulse and dynamism.

Present day pro-Europeans owe a lot to the Federalists. The establishment of the Coal and Steel Community in 1950 that created a supranational 'High Authority' (from which emerged the European Commission) was the direct result of Jean Monnet's personal experience of the failures of undiluted intergovernmentalism in the inter-war years when, in the League of Nations, one country's veto could block all progress on anything, however trivial. The genius of the Spaak Committee's work, which led to the Common Market and the Treaty of Rome in 1955-7, was to recognise that a free trade area alone was not politically attainable without other common policies that would guarantee a sense of equity between the participating countries. Those who today want to turn Europe into a free trade area without all the Brussels baggage should remember this lesson of history. Without a Commission and Court of Justice to enforce the free market rules, and without common policies that balance their effects, the Single Market which accounts for 60 per cent of Britain's trade would neither have existed in the first place nor would it survive the political filleting that the Eurosceptics so ardently desire.

The paradox of the Federalists' early successes is that they created the conditions for the revival of the nation state in Europe, shorn of its nationalistic nastiness in a spirit of genuine reconciliation. France recovered its sense of self-respect in its *'trente glorieuse'*. Italy transformed itself from the third-world rural poverty that nineteenth-century nationalism had never addressed to a first-world modern industrial country within little more than a generation. As did Spain, while becoming a stable democracy after 40 years of Francoism. Above all, a new democratic Germany was welcomed back into the family of nations with a commitment to the European Union as the essence of its being. We take all of this for granted now. Eurosceptics fail too to notice the significance of the European Union now embracing the new democracies of Central and Eastern Europe. Poland, Hungary, the Czech Republic and the rest have not joined the European Union to put themselves under the control of a centralised Brussels super state, having, less than 15 years ago, won their freedom and independence from the iron grip of the former Soviet Union.

So the new Europe is a Union of nations working together in the unique framework of co-operation and integration. It is this hybrid of internationalism and supra-nationalism that characterises the European Union.

If the Constitutional Treaty did indeed mean the creation of a centralised super-state, how very different its content would need to be. It would have had to do far more to strengthen Brussels' powers. Superstates have big federal budgets and levy federal taxes; they have their own army, navy, air force and nuclear deterrent. The EU does not and there is nothing in the Constitution to make that possible or suggest it will ever happen. The Commission would need to be far more powerful than the circumscribed Executive role laid out for it in the Constitutional Treaty. It is clearly not the Government of Europe, nor the sole body with executive power. The European Council, representing the democratically elected heads of government of each country sets the strategic direction of the Union. The Commission retains the right of initiative, but it does not dispose and, under the Constitution, the Commission will do its proposing within the framework set by the European Council. Instead of making the President of the Commission the head of an all-powerful and undisputed Executive, the Constitutional Treaty creates two new positions in the Union – the permanent five-year (as opposed to six-monthly rotating) Presidency of the European Council and the so-called 'European Foreign Minister', both of which are accountable directly to the Member States.

Of course, the Constitutional Treaty strengthens some elements of supranationality. Majority voting on more subjects is necessary to avoid paralysis in a Union of 25 members. The Single Market could not work without it, nor would the CAP ever be reformed or the Doha Trade Round agreed. In areas such as terrorism, international crime, people trafficking and asylum abuse, the problems are bigger than any European country can tackle effectively on their own and the need for common European action is urgent and in the national interest.

Of course 'Brussels' can be, and is too often, a source of bureaucratic stupidity and unwanted interference. The answer to that problem is the fresh air of democracy. More open law-making. A more political Council of Ministers with stronger leadership. A European Parliament with real powers to hold the Commission to account. National Parliaments with rights to call in question new proposals for legislation from the Commission, if they are unnecessary. A legally enforceable Charter of Rights for citizens which enables them to call the European institutions to account for abuses of power, but does not extend EU competence or override national laws. The Constitution helps in all these respects: it is very odd to regard more openness, more democracy, a bigger role for Parliament and more citizens' rights as stepping stones to a centralised super-state.

Without the EU, Europe would be back to where it was in the nine-teenth century – competing nation states with no agreed set of rules to manage that competition. This is not to say that Europe would return to fighting wars. That is ridiculous. But it would mean more and more aggravation as countries clashed over trade, money, responsibility for meeting overseas commitments, whom to let in at their borders, and so on. Not a happy legacy to leave our grandchildren. And, of course, as China and India grow into real super-states, and perhaps Russia revives, the squabbling nation states of Europe would be less and less relevant to the future of our planet. This Constitution represents a sensible *modus vivendi* for Europe. It does not fulfil the old Federalist dream, but its defeat must not signal the renewal of the nationalist nightmare.

5 | The New Economic Case for Europe

Pro-Europeans will not win a referendum simply by mounting a defence of the Constitutional Treaty itself, however strong that defence is. The Constitution is simply an instrument. There is no point in campaigning for an instrument unless we show what we want to use it for. We must make a strong and positive case for Europe's future – for the gains that pursuing a progressive European agenda can bring about over the next decade. That means we have to break free of ultra-caution and show how a positive policy for Europe must be an essential complement to New Labour's third term goals of security and opportunity at home. We need to tackle the prevailing myth that Europe will threaten Britain's economic success. Indeed, pro-Europeans need to show why full engagement in Europe would deliver a significant boost to British growth, productivity and public spending – and must be an essential part of a Labour government's progressive ambitions for Britain.

Why the economic case for Europe must be remade

Britain's economic performance has been good since 1997. No one can dispute that. The new economic argument for Europe is that a full commitment to Europe is essential, not just to sustain that good performance but to improve on it, and add to Britain's growth potential over the next decade. We will only get across to the public how Europe can add this extra dimension if social democrats are prepared to challenge what we have allowed to become the false conventional wisdom of our time: that Britain is substantially outperforming Europe and that Britain's closer association with the EU would damage that success.

In Labour circles, there has been too much reluctance to enter this debate because of understandable nervousness in seeming to challenge the central achievements of the government's economic record. This nervousness has to be overcome. We can honestly boast that Britain's economic performance has improved, but there is room for legitimate debate about the degree of Britain's relative improvement. On this point, the Treasury's own analyses speak for themselves.

Getting this argument right depends on rethinking the economic and social case for Europe. So how should the economic argument for Europe be remade?

First, the acutely British problem of how to achieve growth without inflation – the issue that haunted progressives from the 1950s onwards – appears to have been resolved. We have done it ourselves – though the external shock provided by ERM membership in the early 90s clearly helped. Europe can no longer be sold to the British people on the basis that there is no alternative. This particularly affects the way in which pro-Europeans make the case for the Euro. The case for eventual British membership must now stand or fall on the basis that it will enhance stability and the underlying conditions for growth, not on the grounds that it offers an alternative to successive British government failures of economic management. Contrary to popular perceptions, the Treasury's own Economic Assessment shows that this case stands up to robust analysis, so long as the initial conditions for entry can be got right. Frankness on this issue in the Constitutional referendum will lay the basis for later success on the Euro.

Second, Britain's recent track record on growth is solid but mixed. Certainly, the British are no longer sliding down the European league tables, as we undoubtedly were in the 60s and 70s. Instead, there has been some catch up. But, apart from Germany and Italy, our growth rate has been roughly the same as the rest of Europe's in the last five years –

other countries as diverse as Sweden and Spain have performed better. Crucially, in the British case, there has not been much overall catching-up in productivity per hour. Growth has been achieved by a rising labour force – partly the result of higher employment participation and partly the result of immigration – that works significantly longer hours than the Continental average.

Third, like it or not, labour market flexibility has been a huge plus for Britain. The Labour record in taking us back to virtual full employment has been remarkable – and far more successful than anyone dared to dream of a decade ago. True, at the bottom end of the labour market, there remain acute problems of long-term inactivity, insecurity and bad working conditions. Child poverty has been reduced but more fundamental inequalities, deeper than in many other European countries, remain intractable. Labour's third term needs to do more to combat the wastage of social and economic opportunity that this represents.

Pro Europeans have to develop a clear position on the European Social Model. There is no need for British social democrats to swallow hard, confess that our previous infatuation with the Rhineland model was incorrect and accept that the Thatcherites, after all, were right. The true picture is more nuanced. Britain's low productivity will never be tackled without moving towards Continental levels of social investment. We lack infrastructure. Our workforce lacks skills. We have tolerated far higher levels of marginalisation and social exclusion, with the consequence that a huge reservoir of potential talent is wasted or written off. These are the social challenges New Labour has been trying to address since 1997.

At the same time, the 'core' Europe social model has run into serious difficulties. The German social model was built on the back of an outstandingly productive export economy which could afford high minimum standards of pay and conditions, set by industry-wide agreements. Welfare benefits, financed by employer based insurance, became exceptionally generous. While today, Germany's international competitiveness remains remarkably strong, its manufacturing labour force has shrunk and lower-skilled jobs have been outsourced to Eastern Europe. The growth of the service economy has been held back by a combination of bureaucratic over-regulation, lack of consumer confidence and the high cost of employing low-skilled labour. Unemployment remains stubbornly high as a result of high social benefits, too little condition- ality and poor incentives to seek alternative work: weaknesses that the Red-Green coalition's courageous Hartz reforms are now seeking to address. These problems are most acute in the old East to which the German social model was extended on unification, but without the productive economic base to lend it support, but they are echoed in the old West. Other labour markets in 'core Europe' are beset by similar problems.

So 'Core Europe' needs to accept more labour market flexibility – in particular, stronger work incentives for the unemployed (where New Labour tax credits offer a model to be emulated); welfare-to-work-type benefit conditionality; a lower tax and insurance burden on lower paid jobs; more decentralisation of pay setting and less rigid hiring and firing rules. These realities pose a huge challenge to social partnership and trade unions on the Continent. Their task is to support and manage difficult but unavoidable reforms; not to impose vetoes that can only damage the long term interests of working people and the socially excluded labour market outsiders. In Germany there are signs that in many big corporations the social partners are rising to this challenge.

When we speak of Europe, we need to present a balanced picture. The choice for Britain is not between a 'flexible' Anglo-Saxon model and a 'rigid' Continental model. Flexibility and social investment need to go together. British flexibility and the Rhineland model need to converge. There is a workable alternative to full engagement with Europe. We see it today, warts and all, and it is not one I think social democrats should advocate. We can manage outside the Euro – though we may gradually lose out from new inward investment. We can maintain low inflation without joining the single currency; but, in targeting interest rates at inflation, we have to let the pound find its own level on the exchange markets and allow the trading sectors of our economy that sustain many high quality jobs to bear the brunt of the pain. We could probably manage for a while with a more detached relationship from the EU as a whole without the shock horror of millions of jobs lost. We can achieve strong growth but only by relying more heavily on the long hours economy than our partners. We can sustain high employment but, as labour markets tighten, only by increasing labour market flexibility in one form or another. When our success on employment is so dependent on low wage, low productivity jobs, there are strict limits to the degree of labour market re-regulation that can safely be contemplated.

Some of our European partners have achieved as good or better labour market performance than Britain with less inequality. The Nordic countries have invested in comprehensive childcare; the Dutch in flexi-security, where a proper framework of rights for part-time workers has led to a massive expansion of part-time work. Labour-market flexibility comes in different shapes and sizes: it does not automatically mean the degree of low productivity, insecurity, marginalisation and child poverty that we still experience in Britain, despite Labour's efforts since 1997 to turn the tide. So the Lisbon strategy of economic reform is not about 'us' telling 'them' to become Anglo-Saxon. It is about essential reforms all round in order to modernise the European social model and create something that works – which I would describe as modernised European social democracy. This is not to suggest that labour market and welfare state reforms can or should be imposed at European level, or fitted into some centralised straightjacket, though Brussels can be a useful 'bully pulpit'. We will never benchmark ourselves effectively against our partners' experience unless we are ready to accept that 'core Europe' has some important strengths and that Britain has some devastating weaknesses, not simply vice versa.

How completing the Single Market will boost British productivity and growth

Many people tend to think of the Single Market as something that happened back in 1992 and which, with skilful diplomacy, we could hang on to, whatever happens to Britain's broader relations with the EU. But the single market is a largely incomplete venture, with the biggest advances yet to come. The next decade offers enormous scope for productivity gains and higher growth potential for Britain that would be lost if we are not fully engaged in Europe.

The costs of 'non-Europe' are huge. The academic evidence is overwhelming. European GDP would have been 1.4 per cent lower by 2002 if 1992 had never happened.[23] And the potential future gains are greater still. The extension of the Single Market to Services alone would add 0.6 per cent[24]; the creation of a Single Capital Market in Europe could add 1.1 per cent[25]; the full liberalisation of telecoms and electricity markets would in itself add 0.6 per cent.[26] Of course it would be methodologically incorrect to add up all these separate studies into a single growth gain, but an IMF study in 2003 concluded that realistic competition-friendly product market reforms could add 4.3 per cent to European GDP. Combined with labour market and financial market liberalisation, the combined impact could be as high as 10 per cent.[27]

Talk of this potential is not 'pie in the sky'. There are six policy priorities for deepening the Single Market which only a Labour Government committed heart and soul to Europe can help realise:

1. A Commission crack down on abuse of market power by dominant companies: a strong and single minded Commission has the necessary powers, but needs the political backing of key Member States to use them to the full.

2. Completion of the Doha Trade Round to pull down global trade barriers and open up world markets for developing countries.

3. Full liberalisation of network industries such as Energy, Rail, Telecoms and Posts by implementing in practice what the Lisbon agenda has agreed on paper.

4. Determined follow through of the Financial Services Action Plan to fuse a single capital market in Europe which will cut the costs of borrowing for mortgages and business investment across the EU.

5. Opening up of the cross border market in Services on the basis of the recently proposed Services Directive. Commitments to liberalisation of services, which now account for over 70 per cent of GDP, have been made; now, while taking account of the special position of sensitive public services, they have to be delivered.

6. Further liberalisation of public procurement, both through tighter enforcement of existing rules by Member States and the inclusion of presently protected sectors.

Some social democrats tend to baulk at these pro Single Market arguments. But it is in the interests of the mass of the population, workers and consumers alike, that social democrats should use the power of government to curb the abuse of monopoly power and promote fair competition.

The case for the Single Market isn't any longer simply about economies of scale, but about tough competition driving innovation and productivity. In the 70s, steelmakers were enthusiastic about the Common Market because of the potential to become competitive with the rest of the world by building bigger plants with lower costs per unit of production. But old concepts can easily get in the way of today's real arguments. A growing business in Britain is in a stronger position if it is able to sell into a 'home market' of 300 million plus, because it can identify where it should specialise and grow a competitive niche. That specialisation, in turn, increases the added value of its products and services. This argument is as relevant to small-growing firms as to big multi-nationals, and as relevant to services as goods. Identifying a profitable niche across a broad integrated market is what enables the growing small and medium-sized enterprise to prosper, and SMEs are the most dynamic source of job creation in the modern European economy.

The left has to acknowledge and respond to the tough reality of a dynamic market economy which is also a significant source of the growth we need. Between 5 and 20 per cent of firms enter and exit the market every year, but 'firms that leave the market are the least productive and their departures contribute more than 20 per cent of the productivity gains' in any one year.[28] Companies constantly downsize and make redundancies as other companies expand and grow. So equipping people for change must also be at the core of a credible social democratic strategy for economic growth.

The new social market: how to adapt to economic change

Social democrats believe in sensible public intervention where markets fail. The extension of the Single Market has been accompanied by rafts of environmental, consumer and social legislation. While Eurosceptics object to this as 'over-regulation', should social democrats? It is, of course, a legitimate concern to ensure that regulation does not damage competitiveness or destroy jobs. That is why the UK has been right to press for greater commitment to 'better regulation' within the EU. But for social democrats, the degree of regulation is a question of balance and pragmatism, not principle: a sustainable social market economy requires an underpinning of necessary regulation. That is one excellent reason why the EU is a good thing, not a bad thing. Does anyone believe that a British government of any Party label would have provided such a comprehensive framework of legislation to underpin a sustainable social market economy, had the European Union not been in existence or Britain not been part of it?

The key question to ask is: 'what should sensibly be done at European level?' Welfare systems and labour markets are national and distinctive. Economic intervention generally works best when it is as close to the ground as possible. Social democrats should not advocate a role for Brussels that it cannot adequately fulfil. It is right to be cautious about massive new spending programmes at European level or uniform approaches that do not account for national and regional diversity. But we should be more confident in arguing the case for more Europe to promote a sustainable knowledge economy and tackle market failures at European level where EU action can add real value to national efforts.

Europe's knowledge economy deficit with the United States is huge. On higher education, the EU spends 1.4 per cent of GDP; the United States around 3 per cent. On R&D, the EU spends 1.8 per cent of GDP; the United States 2.7 per cent. On both measures, Britain is around the EU average, despite the Government's efforts on the research budget and university tuition fees, indicating the scale of the knowledge deficit that the Conservatives left behind. The economic benefits of increased knowledge investment across Europe are estimated to be huge. A permanent increase in Europe's actual school leaving age by one year would increase the long run productivity growth rate by 0.45 per cent; a permanent 1 per cent increase in the share of national wealth devoted to R&D would increase the long term growth rate by 0.6 per cent every year.[29]

European spending programmes should be focused on the creation of European centres of research excellence, and building technology platforms that link in with European companies. Business conceives its innovation policies on a European scale, but research remains both compartmentalised on national lines and too distant from business. We need bigger European incentives to promote researcher mobility, intellectual exchange and higher academic rewards within the EU in order to counter the transatlantic brain drain and attract the world's highest talent to Europe.

Europe's top social priority should be to help workers adapt to the more rapid economic change that a combination of deeper market integration and increased supply side investment will bring. Labour market and welfare reforms are essentially national responsibilities, though European-level benchmarking and peer pressure has helped to build the present reform consensus.

But Europe has an instrument of its own to promote social cohesion in the shape of Structural Funds. These should be modernised rather than scrapped. The new Member States have a huge deficit of traditional infrastructure investment to overcome. But in the EU 15 there is an emerging 'social gap' that a new imaginative European programme could fill. While Member States have their own systems of schooling, further and higher education, and vocational training, what is pretty universally absent is a comprehensive package of assistance for workers in mid life faced with economic restructuring, to help both with full skill retraining and mobility. Doing this through a pan-European scheme which would facilitate economic adjustment, and compensate redundant workers for their retraining costs, makes logical sense. If individual Member States attempted to impose arduous retraining obligations on employers who make workers redundant, they could put off new investment or lead to 'social dumping', as plants were closed in member States where the legal obligations to redundant workers were lighter.

The greatest European market failure of all is one of economic policy co-ordination within an integrated economic area. Euroland has a single monetary policy, but no co-ordinated fiscal policy to balance and match it. As a result, growth fails to achieve its full potential, structural reform becomes more politically difficult than it otherwise would be, and we all lose out, including Britain, despite our self exclusion from the Eurozone. Anti-Europeans argue that we surrender a key dimension of national sovereignty if we agree to any form of 'fiscal federalism'. There is no issue here of national sovereignty over spending and tax levels, which must remain questions for national decision. What is at stake is a common approach to the level of budget deficits that Member States are allowed, and whether the rules for this common approach are sensibly framed. The Stability & Growth Pact's rules have placed arbitrary limits on deficits that ignore the economic cycle but at long last there is an emerging consensus for reform. Carrying this through will remove one of the most potent anti-European bogeys in the referendum campaign.

How closer European integration can boost British growth and public spending

Closer ties to Europe are an essential framework condition for higher growth and higher public spending. Turn our back on Europe and we suffer a needless sacrifice of growth potential and a sacrifice of social democratic ambition. Faster economic growth that facilitates redistributive public expenditure was at the heart of Crosland's social democratic thinking in the 1950s. It has been the essence of our New Labour government's practice of power since 1997. Spending on hospitals will have grown by 90 per cent in real terms under ten years of New Labour by 2007/8. On schools, it will have grown 60 per cent. Good economic management has facilitated this. But we know we are coming up against the limits of rapidly rising public spending pretty soon, if further large tax increases are to be avoided. A full commitment to the European project, which raises our productivity and growth potential, can help ease the domestic tax constraint on British social democracy.

The scale of the economic benefits that deeper European integration offers is potentially huge. The flawed degree of integration provided by the present Single Market amounts to a missed opportunity of a £15-£20billion increment to British national wealth every year. That also means an extra £6-£8billion of public spending, which would not otherwise be available without higher taxes. Radical deepening of the Single Market, together with effective action to tackle Europe's knowledge economy deficit, will greatly enhance those benefits.

But there's even more to come if in due course Britain joins the Euro. Last year's Treasury assessment estimated that Euro membership could raise Britain's annual growth potential by a quarter of 1 per cent. As

Tony Blair pointed out in his July 2003 speech in Tokyo: 'the magic of compound interest means that after 30 years the nation garners an annual benefit of between 5 per cent and 9 per cent of GDP [every year]'. That amounts to the whole annual cost of the NHS. The increment to growth would be more than enough to satisfy Labour's medium term ambitions for universal childcare, a proper system of lifelong learning, a high basic state pension and the abolition of child poverty. So it is no minor matter.

There is more than the potential for faster productivity growth to commend a reformed Europe as a successful social democratic growth model. The Single Market has already proved crucial to the UK's attractiveness as a base for long-term investment. Within the Euro we could do better still. Think of the type of overseas investment that has flooded into Ireland, contributing to an extraordinary growth performance. Within little more than a generation, this has transformed an agricultural and clerical backwater into one of the most dynamic countries in Europe, and one which now enjoys a higher standard of living than our own. Until recently, there was more US investment each year in the tiny Republic of Ireland than in the whole of China. Of course, several factors have contributed to Ireland's success – a very favourable business tax regime; the success of Irish education; the commitment of successive US Administrations to the Northern Irish Peace Process; and the English language. But, if one asks why Ireland has done so well, a significant element of the answer must be the Single Market and the Euro.

Attracting inward investment is crucial to Britain, given that few large British companies are world beaters in modern manufacturing. Long-term inward investment is a crucial driver of high-tech, high-skilled jobs. Without it, we miss out on the quality of jobs created, the quality of skills and infrastructure fostered, and the quality of management raised. These are all qualities Britain needs to close the productivity gap with our European partners. Without inward investment, nothing will brake the growing polarisation in the British labour market: accelerating rewards for high performers at the top and low-paid, low-productivity service jobs at the bottom.

If we became more confident in arguing the economic and social benefits that flow from the Single Market, then the case for the Euro would follow logically and technically on from this. While an independent Bank of England can control inflation, pound sterling is left to find its own level. There is no guarantee that the level of the pound will be 'right' for those who trade overseas or face overseas competition. Currency markets are subject to bubbles and huge swings above and below fundamental values; on this, Keynes's prejudices are still relevant. As long as we stay outside, the risks and uncertainties around rates of return on long-term investment in the UK will be greater than in the Euro area. As a result, the structure of our economy is biased towards trading activities that do not involve large fixed and costly investments. The economy is more inclined to live in the short term and live on its wits. This is something that British services have excelled in, but I am not confident that Tony Crosland would have thought this outcome good for jobs in Grimsby.

The progressive agenda: a market economy with social justice

Some on the British left may baulk at this social democratic characterisation of the European project, and see nothing distinctively progressive or social democratic in the arguments I have made for more liberalisation, more competition and more market integration. But Europe offers the only viable framework for a social democratic vision of sustainable growth within a social market economy.

There is a long Labour tradition, dating back to the 1950s, of seeing Europe as a constraint on growth and a constraint on socialist ambition. For many then on the left, Europe was a conservative, capitalist conspiracy. It offended against the central idea of British socialism that central planning, in some ill-defined shape or form, was the route to faster growth and greater social justice. The Attlee government may have made a huge historic error in rejecting the Schumann Plan in 1950-51, but their mistake was understandable. Herbert Morrison, in signing off Britain's 'No' at the Ivy Restaurant, quipped: 'The Durham miners won't wear it'. It was not just the power structures of the Labour Party he had in mind, but a political and ideological mind-set. To put the British coal and steel industries under the control of a supranational authority was unthinkable at a time when these industries employed some million and a quarter people and had just been taken into public ownership – in the case of the mines, after decades of brutal class struggle. They were the 'commanding heights' of the economy, and Labour believed their future had to be planned.

Today's Labour Party has a deeper understanding of the role of markets, and takes a different view of central planning from the 1950s. The revision of Clause Four in 1995 put an end to half a century of confusion between ends and means. We believe that markets can be put at the service of the public interest. And, once we go along with that proposition, logic suggests that we should aim for markets that work as efficiently as they possibly can within a framework that safeguards the public interest. Full engagement with the European Union is the best way to achieve this. While you can be fully committed to the European Union without being on the political left, progressives need to realise that there is no viable modern social democratic project for Britain outside Europe.

6 | The Progressive Response to Globalisation

What is Europe's role in the age of globalisation? As anonymous global forces challenge the power and sovereignty of nation states, the New Case for Europe should command a wide consensus. Isn't it obvious that we should try to recapture at least some of our diminished sovereignty by acting together as Europeans, especially with the coming shift in the balance of world power to Asia? Neo-liberals may not agree – having little belief in the power of politics to shape globalisation – but surely any social democrat has to believe that they are simply wrong-headed.

Instead of hesitating nervously about Europe's developing role in the world, British social democrats should be in the vanguard of the argument for Europe as a force for good in managing globalisation. But an influential section of British opinion will not accept this. In their eyes, we may trade with the rest of Europe but we share a fundamentally different tradition of values across the Atlantic. This highlights the fundamental tough choice which Britain now faces about our role in the world. Only by breaking with the 'special relationship' illusions of the post-war period can Britain play a pivotal role in shaping the new transatlantic relationship between the EU and an internationalist United States which will do so much to shape the world order progressives want to see.

Europe and the battle over globalisation

Anti-Europeans are using globalisation to mount a fresh attack on Europe. Their arguments are given such wide coverage that we cannot afford to leave them in peace to write their columns in the Murdoch press and European edition of the *Wall Street Journal*. Here, globalisation becomes shorthand for the dynamism of the United States and the rise of Asia, making European integration at best an irrelevance and at worst an obstruction to achieving globalisation's full potential. Britain, on this view, would be best advised to steer well clear of a Europe allegedly hooked on over-regulation and harmonisation, and to stick with its 'special relationship' with a United States with which we share common political values and interests.

At the other end of the spectrum, some on Europe's left define their economic policy by anti-globalisation and their foreign policy by anti-Americanism. They are wrong. There may be a short term political gain in defending existing industrial structures, but the risk is that this degenerates into populist gestures that berate inward investors for daring to close factories, obstruct takeovers of popular national champions and make loud complaints about the dangers of 'delocalisation'. This can only be negative for Europe's growth potential. Equally misguided is the demand for harmonisation of corporate taxes in the hope of stemming the flow of lost jobs to low-tax, low-wage parts of the enlarged Union. Some elements of the left still think that it is possible to protect workers against industrial change by imposing regulatory requirements on businesses that 'protect jobs'. This can only damage Europe in a world of mobile capital. The evidence strongly suggests that Europe has far more to gain than to lose from the free flow of both inward and outward investment, though some groups of workers are bound to lose out. The answer to these pressures is not for Britain to turn its back on Europe, but for British social democrats to win the battle for a modern response to globalisation. This requires a firm rejection of protectionism at home and abroad.

A balanced approach to harmonisation

Some EU reformers couple their rejection of protectionism with a blanket rejection of tax and social harmonisation within the EU itself. But there is too much ideology in this. Following the latest enlargement, only a minority within the EU support the Eurosceptic spectre of a centralised, harmonised, protectionist super state. There can be no objection in principle to a framework of a minimum social standards at EU level (which largely exists already as a result of the Social Chapter), but only to specific measures that may over constrain flexibility and have unintended consequences in lost jobs.

Similarly in the field of tax, social democrats should adopt a pragmatic approach. VAT rules are already harmonised and Britain has played the leading part in shaping the EU Savings Directive. There are some other obvious examples of where action on tax may be desirable at European level. National sovereignty in setting excise duties is in practice limited if citizens can bring in cigarettes and liquor in huge quantities from other EU countries at lower rates of duty, as they do, with huge losses to the UK Exchequer. Business would obtain significant costs savings if there was a harmonised corporate tax base across the EU – the rates could still vary between countries but the regulatory burden on business would be much reduced. And some environmental taxes can only sensibly be levied on an EU basis, for example a tax on aviation fuel, which is highly desirable to reduce harmful emissions that are a major source of climate change, and would be a new source of funding for European overseas aid and the International Financing Facility.

Tax competition in the last ten years has brought benefits in terms of greater EU competitiveness, but no social democrat could believe that a 'race to the bottom' within the EU would be desirable, affecting as it would our ability to fund essential public services. In debating tax issues, social democrats need to think through the limitations of national sovereignty and argue for the practical benefits of EU co-operation in tax on a case by case basis.

Europe as a progressive force for good in the world

The progressive agenda for Europe's future should be to build on the EU's current influential role in trade, and widen the EU role in the international financial institutions, development aid and nation building/peacekeeping.

On trade, it is seriously misleading to characterise Europe as protectionist when the EU has been the leading force for trade liberalisation in successive trade rounds. Uniquely, in trade, Europe has been a credible partner of the United States. Competence over trade is one of the few 'exclusive' competences of the Union, where the Commission has negotiating authority on the Member States' behalf. Those Brits who think that 'sovereignty pooling' is all bad should ponder how difficult trade agreements would be if the French Government retained national sovereignty over trade and could exercise a national veto. Our progressive hopes for trade justice and the Doha Round depend on the EU's ability to mobilise a constituency for open trade that takes account of the special needs of the developing world. The EU's August announcement of its readiness to phase out agricultural export subsidies shows that reform, although difficult, can be achieved.

Indeed, it is a free trade Europe which prevents the United States going protectionist. Protectionism is a far bigger risk in the United States than in Europe, because the absence of an effective social safety net makes it very difficult for American industrial workers to accept industrial change. As progressives, we can only have sympathy with their plight when losing a job means loss of health insurance and pension rights, combined with the complete absence of unemployment pay in many States for able-bodied males. Paradoxically, the much-despised European social model makes it easier for workers to accept redundancy and makes trade liberalisation more politically feasible. That model needs modernisation, not abolition, to equip people better for a world of more rapid change.

Europe needs to build its global influence by playing a greater role in the international financial institutions. Eurozone members are beginning to co-ordinate their positions in the IMF and World Bank, where their combined voting weight exceeds that of the United States. Some day, this will end in a single Eurozone seat as the Bretton Woods institutions are reformed to give the new economic powerhouses of the world in Asia and South America proper representation. Britain will join in this process of integration if and when we join the Euro – the sooner the better, as our influence will gradually be squeezed between the power blocks of the Euro, Dollar, Yen and Chinese Renimbi. This matters, not only to burying the discredited 'Washington consensus', but in managing more successfully the painful adjustments that the changing balance of economic power in the world and more open trade will impose on some of the most vulnerable countries.

Take some current examples where this matters: Bangladesh is about to suffer an economic hurricane, threatening millions of jobs, as the quotas come off textile imports with the Chinese textile industry expected to take half of the world market. Similarly the necessary reform of the protectionist EU sugar regime will bring jobs to countries like Brazil but risks destroying the economic base of poor Caribbean countries that currently receive preferential access to EU markets. These countries need immediate help from the IMF in order to manage the shock to their balance of payments, and long-term help from the World Bank to restructure their economies. The EU must use its united clout to make sure this happens – and that requires single EU representation.

Third, development aid. Africa and climate change are Tony Blair's declared priorities for Britain's Presidency in 2005 of both the EU and the G8. Britain and France have this agenda in common as the fading rivalries of Europe's one-time colonial powers give way to common policies co-ordinated through the EU. No one would say that this is working perfectly. By common consent, the British run far more effective overseas development programmes than the EU. However, the EU Development budget is the largest in the world, so pooling policy instruments within a reformed EU framework makes overriding long-term sense if we want to maximise impact and influence, and eliminate costly administrative duplication. The Millennium Goals will not be met without a dramatic step change in levels of aid. Gordon Brown's imaginative proposal for an International Financing Facility to dramatically front load the development assistance that the rich nations of the world offer the poor could make the vital difference. If the US and Japan won't play ball, then why not achieve at least a good part of this dramatic increase in development assistance through the EU, by allowing the EU to issue Development Bonds on the world financial markets with the interest financed by equitable contributions from Member States?

Fourth, nation building capabilities. The EU should develop greater capacity for civilian and military intervention. After Iraq, anti-Europeans sneer about Europe's capacity for united action. Yet, other than on Iraq, the recent European record shows them to be wrong. There is coherence and full acceptance of European responsibility in the Balkans, where there was chaos in Europe's approach a decade ago. We have also seen successful Anglo-French military intervention in central Africa to avert the risk of another Rwanda style genocide. The only practical support that the Palestinian authority can count on has come from the EU. The priority must be to build up the EU's intervention capacities in a practical way.

Is a new transatlantic partnership possible?

But how should Europe deal with America? Some British pro-Europeans believe that the end of the Cold War has pushed Europe and America fundamentally apart. In their view, we need a more united Europe to stand up to George Bush and US unilateralism – and they despair that Tony Blair could not and would not make this argument in a referendum campaign. But there is an argument Blair can make which is more credible. The best progressive case for Europe is that only a more cohesive Europe can offer the credible prospect of a more equal and effective partnership with America.

The old cement of Atlanticism has loosened. There are no longer Soviet tank divisions within a few hundred miles of the English

Channel. But new threats to our peace and security are not figments of the imagination. The threat from terrorism is real. Instability in the Middle East is as much of a threat to Europe as to the United States, arguably more so because the Middle East is on our own doorstep. Europe is more at risk from the illegal flow of people, drugs, terrorism and WMD. There remains a large area of common ground of shared interests between Europe and America, even if one feels uncomfortable about the idea of sharing values with the socially conservative half of American society.

For the new Europe, multipolarism is a dangerous delusion. There is no way an alliance of the EU, Russia and China could be a stable counterweight to a unilateralist United States. There are no shared values that would underpin such a combination – neither individual liberty, political freedom nor respect for minorities. Such a strategy would not enhance European security but only put it at risk by alienating the United States and dangerously reinforcing Russia's residual 'great power' psychology. Nor must we fall into the trap of seeing the US as the problem in the modern world, even if we disagree with the US conduct of policy in particular instances. On the left one hears the mantra: without America, no globalisation; without globalisation, no causes of terrorism or terrorism itself. This slippery slope leads logically to the amoral conclusion that the United States itself must bear the blame for 9/11. We should avoid going there.

The question on both sides of the Atlantic is whether the aspiration to a more equal partnership with a new common purpose is at all realistic. We know what the common agenda of this new Atlantic partnership should be: to tackle terrorism and, with equal determination, take forward a broader agenda of tackling its 'causes'. There is also a compelling logic: the US needs the EU, both militarily – to help rebuild failed States – and politically and economically – as a capable partner in tackling terrorism's root causes.

The question is not whether the EU should seek partnership with the United States. The progressive answer must be that we should. The really uncomfortable question is whether the US wants a meaningful partnership with us – and if they might, how do we make the possibility attractive.

In the Bush Administration, we have seen an undercurrent of impatience with multilateral institutions and approaches, even when the Administration has sought to pursue them. The doctrine that the 'mission determines the coalition' asserts that the US will seek allies for whatever it wants to do – but only on its own terms. Some Republican conservatives rejoice in this view and want America to pursue a policy of divide and rule to entrench the Rumsfeld division between 'Old' and 'New' Europe. Voices within the Heritage Foundation and American Enterprise Institute oppose the Constitution on the grounds that it ties the British into Europe too much. They have only contempt for those nations of Europe which they see as useless posturers, lacking the power and will to act, and want to separate Britain off from Europe so that the US's most loyal ally can act in their support without inhibition. Yet a substantial and influential body of US opinion – not exclusively Democrat – does not share the unilateralist conception of America's role in the world. And post-Iraq the body of opinion which thinks internationalism a better bet than unilateralism is growing. Even supreme military force and technological hegemony have their limits.

How could Europeans take the opportunity to engage the Americans in any kind of renewed partnership? To make this vision work, Europe would have to get much more serious, first, about recognising the seriousness of the threats that Europe faces, and second, about developing its own capabilities. Here one is forced to be sceptical, though not pessimistic. Iraq has left major bruises. On the positive side, the French are a major military power, not imbued with pacifism, while the Germans are at heart natural transatlanticists, keen for American support for a German permanent seat on the Security Council. On capabilities, one senses that the psychological moment is ripe for a major breakthrough in force modernisation and capability pooling. The Constitution will help facilitate this, if the will is there.

But it is the British, above all, who hover uncertainly, half in and half out: supporting the development of an EU military staff, but not one that disturbs US susceptibilities within NATO; developing EU battle-groups, but reluctant to pool the logistical supply chain that might produce some of the savings in defence duplication to enable troops in the front line to be properly equipped; open to joint procurement, but without a clear policy for the future of the European defence industry. From time to time, Tony Blair has offered a strong lead in taking forward European Defence: without his commitment progress would almost certainly have stalled.

There is an even bigger sense in which Britain's role is pivotal. However, we are curiously unwilling to recognise it because it is not very comfortable for the old assumptions of the special relationship. Britain now faces a fundamental and tough choice about our future role in the world. On the one side, the possibility of a revived Atlanticism, where we throw in our lot unequivocally with our European partners to build a stronger, more effective EU on the world stage. On the other side, we face the awful prospect of a dying Atlanticism, where we tag along behind the United States, but from which the rest of Europe gradually distances itself.

The old model of the 'bridge' needs major reconstruction. Up to now, it's been a bridge across which the traffic has been pretty much all one way. Tony Blair has sought desperately hard to influence US policy for the good behind the scenes. But too often we have presented our European partners with an Anglo-American *fait accompli*. A partnership has to be about more than the British telling the rest of the EU that they have no alternative but to accept the best deal that the UK has been able to cook up on their behalf with Washington.

The key test will be how Britain in future handles its relations with the United States.

Certainly, London should maintain total transparency with our US friends and allies. But Britain must give greater priority to securing agreement with EU partners, even if that means some loss of closeness with the US. It is better in the long run for UK to use its influence to secure a united EU position that can be the basis for effective transatlantic co-operation, than that we should always be the USA's loyal ally at the cost of isolation in the EU.

Both the British and the Americans have to realise that the only basis on which there can be a new transatlaticism is a more equal partnership between a more effective and united EU and a more internationalist America. This is deeply painful and disturbing for those old style Atlanticists – including parts of the British military and diplomatic establishment – who fondly believe we can get NATO back to what it was in its glory days. But it is a flawed sentiment. NATO retains importance. Its Article 5 guarantee is of particular value to new Central Asian and Eastern European democracies which do not regard Russia's future path as automatically or inevitably benign.

The Americans themselves have not shown a great appetite for renewed NATO commitment. They brushed aside George Robertson when after 9/11, as NATO Secretary General, he invoked NATO's Article 5. Now they would like NATO to act more 'out of area', and want to build up its Rapid Reaction capability. But the reality is that unless the French and Germans are more on board, NATO is a pretty broken reed.

So the new global case for Europe is that Britain can act as the pivot of a new and progressive transatlantic partnership, but only if we finally make a radical break with the 'special relationship' illusions that still hang over from the second half of the twentieth century.

Conclusion

So can the battle for the Constitutional Treaty be won? Despite the prevailing pessimism, the answer is an unequivocal 'yes' – if Labour lives up to its historic responsibilities. For now, however, most opinion polls are dreadful. In the absence of any immediate campaign, until at least after the General Election, they may even get worse. But the pro-European position is by no means as hopeless as superficially it appears.

The dominating fact about British public opinion is the low level of awareness of what the European Constitutional Treaty actually is, combined with widespread confusion about what it implies. Analyses tell us that the public has an appetite for genuine objective information, but a suspicion of the political class's ability to provide it. We should be grateful that they are also extremely sceptical about what they read in the newspapers.

The British public, especially in England, is torn between rival fears. On the one hand, a fear that our sense of identity will be diluted and lost, in all manner of ways that the Constitution does not in reality threaten. In a high profile referendum, the pro-Europeans will have the opportunity to allay these fears. On the other hand, people fear isolation if the Continent goes ahead without us. The public feel a sense of inevitability about Britain's ties with Europe, on which pro-Europeans can build in a referendum.

In an era of increasing insecurity, where change is seen as more and more problematic, people cling to myths about the past, as symbols of an identity they see as under threat. This is reinforced by the constant media emphasis on the historical image of Britain bravely standing alone against Fascism in the Second World War. This has become the dominant metaphor of how the British people see their role in the world. To counter this, pro-Europeans need to present, in an uncertain and dangerous world, a forward looking vision of Britain's role as a leading player in a Europe whose values and interests we share.

This pamphlet has not been a study of how we win over public opinion to Europe: that is a separate task. It has been about why the Labour Party has got to put its all into this battle. For in the author's view the party cannot afford to lose this fight. The political costs of defeat would be frighteningly high, not only to the authority of a third term Labour Government, not only by giving a tremendous boost to the forces of right wing populism in our country, but by gravely under-mining the fragile progressive consensus on which British social democracy has built its revival since the 1990s. Lose the progressive case for Europe and we weaken severely the progressive consensus in Britain.

To win the Europe referendum will require a mobilisation of opinion across wide sections of British society. We will need non-political people as well as politicians to make the case. We will need all the different pressure groups and interests in our civil society – from trade unionists to environmentalists, from consumer groups to trade associations – to explain to their members and supporters why Europe matters. We will need a precise explanation of what is likely to happen if Britain votes 'No' – that this is not a vote for sudden withdrawal, which is untrue, but that it pushes us down a slippery slope to 'associate membership', where in order to gain continued access to the Single Market we would have to accept rules over which we had no control, whilst losing out on wider political influence in Europe and the world.

But an effective pro-European campaign will never emerge unless Labour offers a lead, and then takes the leading role. The surviving 'big beasts' of the Major/Thatcher jungle still carry some weight with the public, given that few new and convincing Conservative figures have emerged since 1997. But the Tory pro-Europeans are a dying breed. The Lib Dems are a party with a consistent record of pro-Europeanism and a strongly committed pro European leader – but at the grass roots they are increasingly a federation of municipal activists and constituency caseworkers who resent an unpopular commitment to Europe as getting in the way of the next by-election or Council victory. Politically, the referendum campaign depends on Labour.

That requires a determined focus on Europe from Day One of the next Parliament. A key signal would be the appointment of a senior Cabinet Minister in the post election reshuffle to mastermind the planning of the referendum, just as Alan Milburn is masterminding the General Election campaign.

Some people speculate that Labour's own commitment to Europe is also fading: that the conversion to Europe in the late 1980s was always a tactical reaction to Thatcher, not a genuine affair of the heart. In my view this is wrong. A more united, more effective Europe is the best available social democratic project for the age of globalisation. The European Constitutional Treaty should be supported because it embeds progressive centre left values, enhances the prospects for our country of future prosperity with social justice and, in multiplying our influence through Europe, enables Britain to be a stronger force for good in the world. It should also be the occasion for Labour itself to rethink the role of nation state social democracy and reburnish its credentials as a party of a radical constitutional reform. Eight years of power should have convinced the whole Party that we cannot achieve our political objectives by a centralised top down Whitehall approach. Building Europe as an effective vehicle to tackle issues that go beyond the nation state, together with radical decentralisation within Britain, the revival of local democracy and the spread of self governing public service institutions, are all faces of the same die. This is the logic of where Labour stands today. It is an issue of progressivism and modern patriotism in one.

In the campaign itself, pro-Europeans will of course have to explain why legitimate public fears about loss of national identity are misplaced, and that in fact the Constitution makes the Brussels bureaucracy more accountable and puts limits on a centralisation no one wants. The public campaign will inevitably spend much time rebutting the anti Europeans' obsessive falsehoods and deal with legitimate worries and concerns. But social democrats should not confuse their own personal values and convictions with the level of argument that we need properly to make. We should not hang back from arguing a positive progressive case.

General Election night will fire the gun for the start of the European referendum campaign. The Labour Party must be confident of its pro-European values. It must insist the Party's collective leadership stands up for them. It will be time for Labour's pro-Europeans to stand up and make the progressive case.

Notes

1. See Kevin Jefferys, *Anthony Crosland* (Richard Cohen Books, 1999), p.154.
2. Hansard for Tuesday April 20, 2004.
3. Prime Minister's Statement to the House of Commons on the European Council, June 21st,2004.
4. The two most readable accounts of the handling of British policy towards Europe since 1945 are Hugo Young's masterly *This Blessed Plot* (Macmillan, 1998) and Michael Charlton's equally brilliant *The Price of Victory* (BBC Publications, 1983).
5. *Benn Diaries*, Monday December 7th,1970.
6. *Benn Diaries*, Wednesday January 13th,1971.
7. Warsaw, November 2000; Edinburgh, June 2001; Labour Party Conference, 2001.
8. Eurobarometer, October 2003
9. Dimbleby Lecture, November 2003
10. Speech by Francois Mitterand to the European Parliament, 1995.
11. Wolfram Kaiser's *Using Europe, Abusing the Europeans* (Macmillan, 1996) is an immensely stimulating account of Britain and European integration 1945-63 with many contemporary echoes.
12. Philip Stephens' *Politics and the Pound* is the best account, but with the benefit of longer perspective, the significance of our ERM exit grows rather than diminishes.
13. On the Labour side, Giles Radice took precisely this view, as is evident from his diary entry for Sept 16th, 1992, before Britain's forced withdrawal. Giles Radice, *Diaries 1980-2001* (Weidenfeld and Nicolson, 2004).
14. See Roger Broad *Labour's European Dilemmas* (Palgrave, 2001) for a comprehensive account.
15. Sir Alan Budd, Mais Lecture, September 2004.
16. The New Challenge for Europe, Prime Minister Tony Blair's speech at Aachen, May 14th,1999.
17. Stéfan Collignon explains this far more clearly in his book *The European Republic* (Federal Trust, 2003).
18. Laeken Declaration, European Council Conclusions, Dec 2001.

19. *The Making of Europe's Constitution* by Gisela Stuart (Fabian Ideas 609) was published after she ceased to be the British national Parliamentary representative on the Presidium of the Convention that drew up the initial draft of the Constitution. Gisela is entitled to her views, but she did not express them publicly in the Convention itself.
20. Britain has retained special safeguards for its position on border controls (where we have an 'opt out') and criminal procedure (where we can apply an 'emergency brake'), but British pro-Europeans now have the chance to argue that Britain has far more to gain than to lose by being part of common European arrangements.
21. Though in defence, decision making will remain by consensus, even in any core group.
22. Cardiff speech, Nov 2002.
23. European Commission, *The Macro Economic Effects of the Single Market after 10 years* (2002).
24. Copenhagen Economics, *Economic Assessment of the Barriers to the Internal Market for Services* (2004).
25. London Economics, *Of the Macro Economic Impact of Integration of EU Financial Markets* (2002).
26. European Commission, *EU Economy 2002* (2002), Chapter Two.
27. IMF, *World Economic Outlook* (2003).
28. World Bank Development Report (2005), p. 29.
29. European Commission, *EU Economy* (2003).